Empty Nest Transformation

Empty Nest Transformation

The 8-Week System to Rebuild Identity, Create Daily Purpose, and Design Your Next Chapter Without Paralysing Guilt

Lily Wright

Copyright © 2025 Anthony Fallon Publishing

The moral right of the author has been asserted.

All rights reserved.

No part of this publication may be reproduced, stored in a retrieval system, or transmitted, in any form or by any means, without the prior permission in writing of the publisher, nor be otherwise circulated in any form of binding or cover other than that in which it is published and without a similar condition including this condition being imposed on the subsequent purchaser. It is illegal to copy this book, post it to a website, or distribute it by any other means without permission.

First edition

A CIP Catalogue record for this book is available from the British Library

Published by Anthony Fallon Publishing

Paperback ISBN 978-1-0682005-6-4
Hardcover ISBN 978-1-0682005-8-8
E-book ISBN 978-1-0682005-7-1

Also by Lily Wright

STEPPING STONES:
How Progressive Puberty Conversations Build Confident Daughters and Stronger Relationships

The Stepping Stone Approach to Puberty:
How to Create Big Confidence in Growing Boys with Small Talks

Typesetting services by BOOKOW.COM

"The two most important days in your life are the day you are born and the day you find out why."
— Mark Twain.

"We must be willing to let go of the life we planned to have, the life that is waiting for us."
— Joseph Campbell.

Contents

Introduction: The Hidden Opportunity of the Empty Nest		1
1	The Permission Paradox	7
2	Beyond Parent: Your Hidden Identity	14
3	The Time Wealth Paradox	24
4	Your Permission Breakthrough	32
5	The GRANT System: Your Permission Escalation Framework	39
6	Ground: Establishing Your Permission Foundation	46
7	Reclaim: Recovering Small Daily Permissions	57
8	Amplify: Expanding Permission to Meaningful Domains	64
9	Normalise: Integrating Permission into Daily Thinking	73
10	Transcend: Moving Beyond Permission to Entitlement	83
11	Architecting Your Purpose Portfolio	93
12	Relationship Redesign	101
13	Time Architecture Mastery	110
14	Your Legacy Project	121
15	Permission in Professional Reinvention	130
16	Entitled Physical Renewal	139
17	Financial Permission Framework	149
18	Marriage Renaissance Architecture	159
19	Community Contribution Design	168

| 20 | Digital Relationship Architecture | 177 |
| 21 | Navigating Unexpected Transitions | 186 |

Conclusion: From Supporting Character to Author — 198

Appendices: Your Permission-Based Transformation Toolkit — 203

Reader Reviews for "Empty Nest Transformation" — 209

Introduction: The Hidden Opportunity of the Empty Nest

The silence that follows your children leaving home screams with loss and possibility. What happens in that silence, how you interpret it, respond to it, and ultimately transform it, will shape the rest of your life. The empty rooms that once bustled with homework questions, music practice, and teenage drama now stand as blank canvases awaiting your design. This threshold moment demands more than simply adjusting to quieter dinners or fewer loads of laundry.

For many women, the departure of the last child triggers an identity crisis. After decades of organising your schedule, priorities, and even your sense of purpose around your children's needs, you suddenly face days unstructured by school pickups, sports practices, or homework supervision. This shift happens with stunning speed—one day you're planning college visits, and seemingly the next, you're standing in a quiet house wondering who you are now.

"I felt like I'd been laid off from the most important job I'd ever had—with no warning and no severance package," shared Maria, a 52-year-old mother of two who found herself paralysed with indecision six months after her youngest left for university. "My friends told me to 'enjoy the freedom', but I didn't know what to do with it. I waited for someone to tell me it was okay to focus on myself."

This reaction makes perfect psychological sense. For nearly two decades or more, you've trained your brain to prioritise your children's needs, often at your own expense. You've developed profound capabilities as a caregiver, problem-solver, scheduler, mediator, and emotional support system. Those skills didn't vanish when your children moved out, but suddenly, they lack their primary outlet.

What no one tells you about the empty nest is that it contains a disturbing paradox: grief and opportunity arrive simultaneously, creating emotional whiplash. The longing for the busy family home of the past collides with flickers of excitement about potential freedom. This emotional contradiction leads many women to feel guilty about their conflicting feelings—sad when they should be happy about their children's independence, or excited when they think they should be mourning.

The Paradox of Grief and Freedom
The empty nest transition stands apart from other life changes because it combines significant loss with unprecedented opportunity. Unlike retirement, which comes with established social scripts and celebration rituals, or bereavement, which triggers clear support systems, the empty nest exists in an uncomfortable middle ground. Society offers contradictory messages: "Be proud, your job is done" alongside "Don't you miss your kids?" with little guidance on navigating the complex emotional territory in between.

Jennifer, a 48-year-old executive who had scaled back her career to raise three children, described the peculiar nature of this grief: "I found myself crying in my daughter's empty room, then ten minutes later excitedly researching graduate programs I'd always wanted to pursue. Then I'd feel guilty about being excited. It was emotional chaos."

This paradox creates a psychological challenge: how do you honour your genuine feelings of loss while simultaneously exploring the new possibilities? Most empty nesters get stuck in this question, often resolving it by remaining in a holding pattern—neither fully grieving nor moving forward.

The truth that most parents discover only after a prolonged struggle is that the empty nest represents both an ending and a beginning. The question isn't whether you should feel sad or excited—it's how to integrate both emotions into a new understanding of who you are and what comes next.

From Displaced Parent to Transition Architect
The breakthrough that changes everything is a fundamental identity shift: from seeing yourself as a displaced parent to recognising yourself as an architect of transitions.

Your identity was never just "parent." While central and precious, that role expressed something more fundamental about who you are: someone who can design meaningful change, navigate complexity, and create structure from chaos. You've been architecting transitions throughout your parenting journey

—from the newborn phase to kindergarten, from childhood to adolescence, from high school to launching young adults.

Each transition required you to redesign family systems, adjust relationships, and modify your approach while maintaining core values. You didn't just survive these transitions—you orchestrated them with intention and care. This fundamental capability doesn't disappear when your children leave; it remains available to design your next chapter.

Susan, a 55-year-old mother of twins, explained her revelation: "I realised I wasn't just missing my role as Mom—I was missing having something meaningful to build. Once I understood that I could direct that same energy toward creating my next chapter, everything changed. I wasn't just grieving what was gone but hungry to create what was next."

This shift—from mourning a lost role to claiming your identity as an architect of meaningful transitions—provides the foundation for everything that follows. It honours the skills you've developed while redirecting them toward your future.

The Permission Deficit

If you intellectually understand that it's time to focus on yourself but are still unable to move forward, you're experiencing what psychologists call a "permission deficit." After years—often decades—of putting others' needs before your own, your brain has developed deep neural pathways that require external authorisation for self-care or self-focus.

"I knew I should take a class, or join a group, or even just spend time figuring out what I wanted," explained Rebecca, a 49-year-old mother of three. "But every time I tried, I felt this physical discomfort, like I was doing something wrong or selfish. I kept waiting for someone to tell me it was okay."

This permission deficit creates the most common form of empty nest paralysis: you understand intellectually that it's time to prioritise yourself, but emotionally, you remain stuck waiting for authorisation that never comes. Your brain, having been wired through years of parenting to seek external validation for personal choices, continues to search for permission that society isn't structured to provide.

The permission deficit manifests in several common patterns:

- **The Passive Wait**: Putting life on hold until someone explicitly tells you it's okay to focus on yourself.

- **The Hyper availability Loop**: Remaining constantly on-call for adult children to maintain your sense of purpose.
- **The Substitute Caregiving Cycle**: Immediately filling the gap with caring for ageing parents, grandchildren, or others.
- **The Anxiety Spiral**: Endlessly researching options without taking action due to decision paralysis.

None of these patterns leads to genuine transformation. They keep you in a holding pattern—neither fully present in your parenting role nor fully engaged in creating what comes next.

The breakthrough comes in recognising that you are the only one who can grant yourself the permission you're seeking. External validation, while comforting, can't override decades of internal programming. You need a systematic approach to building your "permission muscle" that acknowledges both your right to move forward and the legitimate emotional barriers that make it difficult.

The 8-Week Permission Escalation System

The GRANT Permission Escalation System provides the structured pathway most empty nesters never receive. This revolutionary approach recognises that overcoming permission deficit requires more than just intellectual understanding or motivational advice. It demands a progressive, psychologically sophisticated process that builds your capacity for self-authorisation over time.

The system works through five carefully calibrated stages that build on each other:

Ground: Establish your permission foundation by acknowledging your parenting journey while recognising your right to move forward

Reclaim: Recover small daily permissions by Practising self-authorisation in low-resistance areas that build momentum

Amplify: Expand permission to meaningful domains by applying your growing permission capabilities to identity exploration and key relationships.

Normalise: Integrate permission into daily thinking by creating rituals and environmental cues that reinforce your self-authorisation

Transcend: Move beyond permission to entitlement by recognising your inherent right to self-prioritisation as the foundation for your next chapter.

Each stage builds on the previous, creating a staircase rather than expecting you to leap from permission deficit to complete transformation in a single bound. This incremental approach honours the deep neural pathways created through years of parenting while systematically building new ones.

Over eight weeks, you'll move from tentative first steps to confident self-direction, establishing intellectual understanding and emotional authorisation for your next chapter. The system's power lies in recognising that permission-building is a skill that can be developed systematically rather than a mystical transformation that either happens or doesn't.

Your Next Chapter: From Supporting Character to Author
The empty nest transition offers something precious and rare: the opportunity to move from supporting character to author of your story. After years of facilitating others' growth and development, you can direct that same care and attention toward your unfolding narrative.

This doesn't mean abandoning your role as parent—that connection remains vital and evolves into new forms of relationship. Instead, it means expanding your identity to include new dimensions of purpose, connection, and meaning that complement your ongoing role as a parent to adult children.

Imagine waking up each morning with a clear purpose, structured time, and meaningful connection—all designed around your authentic needs and desires rather than others' expectations. Picture relationships with adult children that balance genuine connection with healthy boundaries, where your wisdom remains valued without creating dependency. Envision a partnership with your spouse that evolves beyond co-parenting into shared adventures and deepening intimacy.

This vision isn't a fantasy. It's the lived reality of empty nesters who've successfully navigated this transition by recognising themselves as architects rather than victims of change. The journey requires courage, structure, and a willingness to challenge deeply ingrained patterns—but the rewards extend far beyond simply "adjusting" to your children's absence.

In the coming chapters, you'll learn how to implement the GRANT Permission Escalation System, building your capacity for self-authorisation one step at a time. You'll discover how to translate your parenting capabilities into new domains, architect meaningful time structures, redesign key relationships, and create purpose that generates daily motivation and significance.

The empty nest isn't the end of your most significant chapter—it's the beginning of the one you get to write yourself. The blank page may feel intimidating now, but with the right tools and framework, it will soon become the most exciting opportunity you've encountered in decades.

In Chapter 1, we'll explore the Permission Paradox—why your brain resists self-prioritisation even when intellectually you know it's time, and how to begin dismantling this barrier to your next chapter.

Chapter 1

THE PERMISSION PARADOX

Sarah's hand trembled as she reached for the doorknob to her daughter's empty bedroom.

Three months had passed since she'd helped Emma move into her college dorm room. Three months of a house too quiet, meals too simple, and time too abundant. Sarah had imagined this day for years—finally having time for her long-postponed dream of painting. She'd even kept Emma's room pristine, thinking she might convert it into an art studio. Yet each time she approached that door with purpose, something stopped her.

Today was no different. Her chest tightened as her fingers touched the cool metal of the doorknob, and her stomach churned with a feeling she couldn't name.

The Day Permission Vanished

"Just open the door, for heaven's sake," Sarah muttered. "It's your house. You're allowed to use this room however you want."

She pushed the door open and stepped inside. Emma's debate trophies still lined the bookshelf. College pennants hung above the desk. The room smelled faintly of the vanilla perfume her daughter had worn throughout high school.

Sarah set down the box of art supplies she'd been carrying and sat heavily on Emma's bed.

"I should feel excited," she thought. "I've talked about having a studio for years. Now I have the time, the space, and even some money saved." She looked down at her hands. "So why does it feel... wrong?"

Sarah didn't Realise that she was experiencing the Permission Paradox—a phenomenon that affects nearly every empty nester. After two decades of putting her daughter's needs first, Sarah's brain had become wired to prioritise others above herself. She would cancel her plans for Emma's school event or her doctor's appointment to attend her daughter's sports practice, and her self-sacrifice would be rewarded with the release of small amounts of dopamine to her brain.

These rewards had created strong neural connections that linked Sarah's identity to caregiving. Her brain had become highly efficient at one crucial calculation: Emma's needs > Sarah's needs.

This wasn't a conscious choice or a lack of self-love. It was a biological adaptation to the demands of motherhood. Sarah's brain had optimised itself for her most important job: raising a healthy, well-adjusted child.

The problem? Those neural pathways don't automatically recalibrate when children leave.

Brain Adaptation	During Active Parenting	Empty Nest Reality
Reward System	Dopamine is released when sacrificing for children	No clear reward system for self-prioritisation
Identity Circuits	Strongly connected to the caregiving role	Weakened connections to personal desires
Habit Formation	Automatic prioritisation of others	No automatic system for self-prioritisation
Decision Making	Simplified by the child-first algorithm	Complicated by a lack of clear priorities

When Your Brain Becomes Your Biggest Obstacle

One week later, Sarah met her friend Maria for coffee. As they settled into a corner table at their favourite café, Sarah noticed the dark circles under Maria's eyes.

"You look exhausted," Sarah said. "Everything okay?"

Maria sighed and wrapped her hands around her mug. "I cancelled my pottery class again. That's three weeks in a row."

"But you were so excited about that class," Sarah said. "You've been talking about getting back into ceramics since Tyler left for school."

"I know, I know," Maria said, frustration edging her voice. "It makes no sense. Tom's at work, Tyler's at college. I have nothing but time. But each Wednesday, as class time approaches, I invent reasons why I can't go."

"Like what?"

"Oh, ridiculous things. Last week, I suddenly remembered I needed to clean out the pantry. The week before, I had convinced myself that I might miss an important call from Tyler, even though he never called on Wednesdays. Yesterday, I just felt... I don't know... guilty."

Maria looked up, her expression a mixture of confusion and shame. "What's wrong with me, Sarah? I should know better than this."

What Maria didn't Realise was that her brain was experiencing a profound conflict between two systems:

1. Her **logical brain** understood that she deserved to take the class, had earned this time for herself, and would benefit from pursuing her interests.
2. Her **emotional brain** sent warning signals—anxiety, guilt, and discomfort—whenever she attempted to prioritise herself.

This wasn't just a matter of "getting over it" or "being stronger." It was a neurological disconnect between what Maria knew intellectually and what she felt emotionally.

Her intellectual understanding said, "I deserve time for myself after decades of caregiving."

But her emotional authorisation system responded: "Warning! Prioritising self-detected! This violates established patterns! Abort!"

This conflict created what psychologists call "permission deficit"—the gap between knowing you should prioritise yourself and feeling truly authorised.

The Surprising Physical Toll of Permission Deficit

Three days after their coffee date, Sarah noticed Maria had sent a text at 3 AM: "You up? Can't sleep again."

Sarah called her friend the next morning. "Another bad night?"

"The worst," Maria admitted. "I lay awake for hours thinking about that stupid pottery class. Part of me is angry that I keep cancelling, and another part feels relieved. How messed up is that?"

"It's not messed up at all," Sarah reassured her. "I'm going through something similar with Emma's room. Yesterday, I got as far as bringing in my art supplies, but then I felt physically ill from the idea of changing anything."

"Exactly!" Maria exclaimed. "It's like my body is fighting against me. Last night, I even had a stress dream. I was in pottery class and kept getting emergency texts from Tyler, but my hands were covered in clay, and I couldn't respond."

What Sarah and Maria were experiencing wasn't unusual. Permission deficit doesn't stay quietly in the mind. It erupts into daily life through physical and emotional symptoms that often seem unrelated to the issue of self-authorisation:

- **Decision paralysis**: Freezing when faced with choices about your own needs and wants
- **Sleep disturbances**: Mind racing with guilt or anxiety when considering personal plans
- **Stomach discomfort**: Physical tension arises when attempting self-prioritisation
- **Sudden busyness**: Unconsciously filling your schedule with low-priority tasks to avoid facing freedom
- **Excessive justification**: Creating elaborate explanations for simple self-care activities
- **Heightened responsiveness**: Jumping at every text from adult children, seeking ways to be needed
- **Procrastination**: Delaying activities focused on your wellbeing despite having time for them

Sarah and Maria discovered they weren't alone at their next book club meeting. Robert, the only man in the group and a former stay-at-home dad, shared his struggle.

"Every time I sit down to write, I get this knot in my stomach," he explained. "I've wanted to write a novel for twenty years, and now I finally have time. But then I remember some urgent errand or household task. Before you know it, the day is gone, and I've written nothing. The weird thing is, when Jake was little, I managed to squeeze in twenty minutes of writing during his soccer practice. Now with all this time, I can't even start."

The group fell silent, recognising their own experiences in Robert's words. Many found that having more time paradoxically made self-focus harder, not easier. The absence of external demands revealed the internal permission deficit, which is typically obscured by legitimate responsibilities.

Jennifer, whose twins had left for college the previous year, nodded vigorously. "I've been getting headaches almost daily since the kids left. My doctor says they're tension headaches, but all the medication in the world doesn't help because the tension comes from inside."

The physical symptoms of "empty nest syndrome" often stem directly from this unrecognised permission deficit:

Common Symptom	Often Attributed To	Related To
Anxiety	Missing your children	Permission deficit triggering stress response
Insomnia	Worry about adult children	Guilt about potential self-focus
Lack of motivation	Depression from loss	Absence of permission for self-directed activities
Irritability	Hormonal changes	Frustration from internal permission conflicts
Fatigue	Ageing or health issues	Energy depletion from constant internal struggle

When Knowledge Isn't Enough

As their book club discussion continued, Jennifer shared a realisation. "You know what's most frustrating? I know I should take better care of myself now that the kids are gone. I've read all the articles about reinventing yourself. I've made lists of things I want to do. But there's this voice in my head saying: 'Who do you think you are?'"

The others nodded in recognition. They all had similar lists. They all understood the concept of self-care. And they all struggled to act on that understanding.

Sarah reached for her notebook. "I think I'm starting to understand what's happening. There's a difference between what we know and feel allowed to do."

She drew a simple diagram and showed it to the group:

Intellectual understanding: Recognising on a cognitive level that you deserve to prioritise yourself.

Emotional authorisation: Feeling in your body and heart that you have permission to act on that understanding.

"Most of the empty nest advice I've read only addresses the first part," Sarah continued. "It tells us what we already know: We should focus on ourselves. We deserve this time. We've earned this freedom."

"But it doesn't touch the deeper issue," Maria added, catching on. "The feeling that we're truly allowed to prioritise ourselves without guilt."

"Exactly," Sarah said. "Without addressing this permission deficit, even the best advice remains theory that we can't implement. It's like having a recipe but being unable to turn on the stove."

Robert leaned forward. "So, willpower alone isn't enough? Because I've been beating myself up for lacking discipline."

"I don't think willpower can override decades of neural pathways," Sarah said. "It's not about being stronger or trying harder. It's about rewiring our brains."

Your Permission Journey Begins with Acceptance

The book club meeting proved transformative for Sarah. Walking home that evening, she reflected on their conversation and felt a weight lifting from her shoulders.

Her struggle wasn't a character flaw or a lack of willpower—it was a predictable result of her success as a parent.

She wasn't struggling because she'd done something wrong. She struggled because she'd done something right: she'd prioritised Emma's wellbeing for decades, and her brain had adapted perfectly to that critical mission.

As her role changed, her brain needed time and specific techniques to adapt to the new reality. Just as she wouldn't expect to excel at a new sport after decades without practice immediately, she couldn't expect to automatically prioritise herself after years of putting others first.

This was why seeking permission to prioritise herself wasn't just normal— it was necessary. The missing piece bridged the gap between what she knew intellectually and felt emotionally authorised to do.

The next morning, Sarah stood again at the door to Emma's room. This time, instead of pushing through her resistance, she acknowledged it.

"I notice I'm feeling guilty about changing this room," she said aloud. "That's my permission deficit talking. It's normal. It doesn't mean I shouldn't move forward—it just means my brain needs time to catch up with my new reality."

She didn't open the door that day. Instead, she went to her desk and wrote "Permission Project" at the top of a fresh page in her journal. Below, she listed small steps she could take to gradually build her permission muscle.

Sarah had taken the first crucial step in her journey: recognising that her permission struggle wasn't a personal failing but a natural response to a significant life transition after decades of other-focused living.

Throughout the following few chapters, you'll learn how Sarah and her friends systematically built their permission "muscles" through what I call the GRANT Permission Escalation System. This five-step framework will help you progressively strengthen your capacity for self-authorisation, moving from small, low-resistance permissions to life-changing authorisations.

However, it's essential to recognise that your struggle isn't a character flaw entirely—it's a perfectly normal response to your situation. By acknowledging this truth, you've already taken the first step toward transforming your relationship with permission.

In the next chapter, we'll explore how your identity was never just "parent" but always included the fundamental capability to architect meaningful transitions. This perspective shift will help you view your empty nest not as an ending, but as the beginning of your next great chapter in life.

Chapter 2

BEYOND PARENT: YOUR HIDDEN IDENTITY

Identity exists beyond roles, waiting silently for rediscovery and recognition. Sarah stood in her daughter's empty bedroom, surrounded by the faint echoes of seventeen years of laughter, tears, and growth. The walls, now bare of posters and photos, seemed to hold the ghosts of conversations past. For nearly two decades, her primary identity had been "Emma's mum." Now Emma was settling into university life 300 miles away, and Sarah felt herself disappearing along with her active parenting role.

"I don't know who I am anymore," she confessed to her friend Diane over coffee the following week. The coffee shop buzzed with morning activity, but Sarah barely noticed. "It sounds dramatic, but it's like someone erased the core of my identity overnight."

Diane nodded, remembering her transition three years earlier. "I felt the same when Jason left. Like I'd been made redundant from the only job that mattered."

"So what did you do?" Sarah asked, wrapping her hands around her mug as if seeking warmth beyond the ceramic.

"I'm still figuring it out," Diane admitted. "But I've stopped thinking of myself as a former parent. I've started seeing myself as someone who's always been good at helping others through transitions. Parenting was just one expression of that."

This sentiment—this feeling of identity extinction that Sarah described—is perhaps the most painful aspect of the empty nest transition. After decades of introducing yourself in relation to your children, making decisions based on their needs, and structuring your time around their activities, the absence of these external reference points can feel like identity erasure.

But this perception is fundamentally flawed.

The Transition Architect Mindset Versus the Vanishing Parent Identity

Mark sat in his car outside his son's college dormitory, keys in the ignition but unable to turn them. The morning had been a blur of unpacking, meeting roommates, and finally saying goodbye. Now, sitting alone in the parking lot, the reality hit him: his daily role as Dad had fundamentally changed.

"Who am I if not Ryan's father?" he thought, surprising himself with the question. Of course, he was still Ryan's father—that wouldn't change. But the active, daily expression of that role had transformed overnight.

Mark moved through his routine in a fog three days after dropping Ryan off. He avoided the kitchen at breakfast time—the empty chair at the table too painful a reminder. He skipped his usual evening walk, previously a time to check in with Ryan about his day. Even watching his favourite shows felt wrong without Ryan's running commentary beside him.

"I feel like I've lost my purpose," he admitted to his wife, Elena, on the fourth night. "I know that sounds crazy. I'm still working the same job, living in the same house, married to the same wonderful woman. But I'm not sure who I am without being Dad daily anymore."

Elena considered his words carefully. "Maybe the problem isn't that you've lost your identity," she suggested. "Maybe it's that you're seeing your identity too narrowly. You weren't just Ryan's dad. You were someone who guided him through every transition in his life—from learning to walk to learning to drive. That capability doesn't disappear just because he's more independent now."

This distinction between seeing yourself as a "vanishing parent" versus recognising yourself as a "transition architect" isn't just semantic wordplay. It's a profound reframing that changes how you approach this new phase.

Your parent identity never existed in isolation—it was always an expression of your deeper capability to architect transitions.

Let's follow Mark's journey as he gradually shifted from the vanishing parent mindset to the transition architect mindset:

Week	Vanishing Parent Thoughts	Transition Architect Realisation
Week 1	"I've lost my purpose now that Ryan doesn't need me daily."	"I've always been good at helping others navigate change."
Week 2	"The skills I developed as a dad aren't useful anymore."	"The patience and problem-solving I developed as a parent apply to many situations."
Week 3	"I need to find a completely new identity now."	"My core identity has always included being adaptable to new phases of life."
Week 4	"Who am I without my son at home?"	"How will I express my capabilities in this next chapter?"

As Mark began to see himself as someone who had always been good at designing and navigating transitions, with parenting just one expression of that capability, his perspective on the empty nest shifted. Rather than seeing himself as a redundant parent, he began to see himself as a transition architect facing a new design challenge: his next chapter.

This shift from seeing yourself as a vanishing parent to recognising yourself as a transition architect is the essential foundation for everything that follows in this book. This isn't about denying grief—the daily absence of your children is a genuine loss that deserves acknowledgement. But it is about recognising that your core capability remains intact and available for this new design challenge.

Identity Archaeology: Excavating Pre-Parenting Passions and Interests

"I don't even remember who I was before I became a mother," Jennifer said, stirring her tea absently. It was her first session with her therapist after both her daughters had left for university within six months of each other. "It's been twenty-three years of being Abby and Zoe's mom. Everything before that feels like it happened to a different person."

"Let's try something," her therapist suggested. "Close your eyes and picture yourself at twenty-two, before children were part of your life. What were you doing that brought you joy?"

Jennifer closed her eyes, struggling at first to conjure an image from so long ago. Gradually, a memory emerged. "I used to write. Poetry, mostly. I'd sit in this little café near my first apartment and write for hours." A smile crossed her face. "I'd forgotten how much I loved that."

"The person who loved writing poetry is still part of you," her therapist pointed out. "She didn't disappear when you became a mother. She just stepped into the background for a while."

Before the all-consuming role of parent dominated your life, you were a person with distinct interests, passions, and pursuits. Those elements of your identity didn't disappear when you became a parent—they were submerged beneath the immediate demands of caregiving.

Think of identity archaeology as the process of carefully excavating those buried aspects of yourself. Not to return to who you were before parenting, but to rediscover elements that might inform who you're becoming now.

Over the next month, Jennifer began her identity archaeology expedition. She found old journals in the attic and spent evenings reading her twenty-something thoughts. She contacted an old friend from her pre-parenting days and arranged to meet for lunch. She even visited that café—still in business after all these years—and brought a notebook.

"I'm not the same person I was before my daughters were born," she told her therapist after four weeks of exploration. "And I wouldn't want to be. But reconnecting with parts of myself that I'd forgotten has helped me see possibilities I couldn't imagine before."

For your identity archaeology process, follow these sequential steps:

Step 1: Recall. Begin by documenting activities, interests, and passions that engaged you before intensive parenting began. Don't censor or judge—list everything you can remember enjoying or finding meaningful.

Step 2: Research. Next, investigate how those interests might have evolved in the intervening years. If you loved photography with a film camera, research how digital photography has transformed the field. If you were passionate about environmental issues, learn about current movements and approaches.

Step 3: Reconnect. Finally, small, experimental steps should be taken to engage with these interests again. Sign up for a one-day workshop, join an online community, or set aside an hour to try an old passion with fresh eyes. Notice what still resonates and what no longer fits.

Jennifer's identity archaeology led her to join a weekly writing group at her local library. "I'm not the same writer I was twenty-five years ago," she reflected.

"My perspective is deeper now. All those years of motherhood have given me so much more to say."

Your archaeology process isn't about returning to the past but about reclaiming valuable artefacts that can inform your future.
One crucial note: This isn't about bypassing grief by rushing to fill the void with old interests. The excavation process should be gentle and curious, not desperate and frantic. You're not digging for a replacement identity but uncovering clues that might inform your evolving self.

Transferable Skills Assessment: How Parenting Capabilities Apply Elsewhere
"I'm starting from zero," Carlos said, his voice tight with frustration. He was sitting across from his career counsellor, six months after his youngest child had left for college. "I've spent the last eighteen years being Dad. That doesn't exactly translate to a compelling CV."

His counsellor, Natalie, looked thoughtful. "Let me challenge that assumption. Tell me about a typical week when your kids were teenagers."

Carlos laughed. "Chaos. Pure chaos. Soccer practice is for Miguel, and debate tournaments are for Isabella. Coordinating who needed the car when, making sure everyone had what they needed for school projects. Managing their social calendars while maintaining some semblance of family dinner time."

"And what happened when plans fell apart—when someone missed the bus or forgot an assignment?"

"We'd problem-solve. Rearrange schedules, call in favours, find workarounds. You do what you have to do."

Natalie nodded. "So, you managed complex logistics across multiple stakeholders with competing priorities. You negotiated conflicts, allocated limited resources, and developed contingency plans when initial approaches failed. Does that sound about right?"

Carlos looked surprised. "I guess I did. I never thought about it that way."

"Those are sophisticated project management and conflict resolution skills," Natalie pointed out. "They translate to professional contexts."

Parenting is perhaps the most sophisticated skill development program ever devised. The capabilities you've developed in raising children represent an extraordinary skill set that applies far beyond the family context. Yet many parents fail to recognise the transferability of these hard-won capabilities.

Over the next month, Carlos worked with Natalie to identify and translate his parenting skills into professional language. He realised that years of helping with homework had made him an excellent teacher and mentor. Navigating his children's social challenges had developed his mediation abilities. Managing the family budget had honed his resource allocation skills.

Three months later, Carlos volunteered at a community centre, teaching financial literacy to teenagers. "I'm using the same patience and explanatory skills I developed helping my kids," he told Natalie. "But now I see these weren't 'just parenting skills'—they're human skills that apply everywhere."

To conduct your own transferable skills assessment, follow this process:

Step 1: Document Parenting Scenarios. List specific parenting situations you navigated successfully. Include everyday routines and unusual challenges. Be specific about what you did and how you approached each situation.

Step 2: Extract Capabilities. For each scenario, identify the underlying capabilities you employed. Did you mediate conflicts? Manage complex logistics? Create systems for the organisation? Teach complex concepts in understandable ways?

Step 3: Translate to New Contexts. For each capability, brainstorm how it might apply in non-parenting contexts. How might conflict resolution skills apply in workplace settings? How might your ability to explain complex topics help in volunteer roles?

Here's how one empty nester translated her parenting capabilities to new contexts:

Parenting Experience	Underlying Capability	New Application
Managing multiple children's schedules	Complex logistics coordination	Event planning volunteer for the community centre
Helping with challenging homework	Breaking complex topics into understandable components	Teaching adult education classes
Resolving sibling conflicts	Mediation and conflict resolution	Workplace team-building facilitator
Managing a family budget during tight times	Resource optimisation and prioritisation	Financial coaching for young adults
Staying calm during teenage crises	Emotional regulation in high-stress situations	Crisis line volunteer

These capabilities represent significant assets in virtually any context. The challenge isn't developing new skills but recognising how your existing capabilities translate to different domains.

Reframing Your Value Beyond Your Caregiving Role

"I feel useless," Mei confessed, barely audible over the restaurant noise. It was her monthly dinner with three friends—all empty nesters at different stages of the transition. "Li calls maybe once a week. Jian texts occasionally. They're building their own lives, which is exactly what should happen, but..."

"But you're wondering what your purpose is now," finished Aisha, who'd been an empty nester for three years.

Mei nodded, blinking back tears. "For twenty years, I've been needed and needed. Now the phone doesn't ring. No one asks what's for dinner or needs help with decisions. It's like I've become invisible."

"I remember that feeling," said Halima, whose twins had left five years earlier. "I defined my value by how much my family needed me. When that suddenly decreased, I felt worthless."

"So, what changed?" Mei asked.

"I had to recognise that my value was never actually based on being needed," Halima explained. "That was just the most visible evidence of my worth. But my value exists independent of my usefulness to others—even my children."

After decades of defining your value primarily through service to others, this concept can be challenging to embrace. But it's an essential shift for moving forward with confidence.

Over the next several months, Mei worked to reframe her understanding of her value. She joined a community garden project, discovering that the nurturing skills she'd developed as a parent applied beautifully to tending plants and mentoring younger gardeners. She took a part-time position at a local bookstore, finding that her ability to recommend the perfect book for a customer's needs drew on the same intuition she'd used to understand her children's unstated feelings.

"I'm starting to see that my value isn't just about being needed by my children," she told her friends six months later. "It's about who I am and what I bring to any situation. That doesn't disappear just because my children are independent."

To begin your value reframing process, consider these principles:

1. **Inherent vs. Role-Based Value:** Your worth exists independent of any role you play. You had value before you became a parent, during active parenting, and now as your parenting role evolves.

2. **Contribution vs. Caregiving:** Your capacity to contribute exists in numerous forms beyond direct caregiving. The same capabilities that made you an effective parent can create value in countless other contexts.

3. **Identity Continuity vs. Replacement:** You're not starting from zero in establishing your value. The capabilities that created your value as a parent remain intact and available for new applications.

4. **Self-Authorisation vs. External Validation:** Your validation no longer needs to come primarily from meeting others' needs. You can now authorise your value through the choices you make and the contributions you choose.

As Mei discovered, embracing these principles doesn't happen overnight. It's a gradual process of recognising your inherent worth beyond your caregiving role. Each small step—whether joining a community project, pursuing education, or simply making choices based on your preferences—reinforces this new understanding of your value.

The Identity Continuity Bridge

One year after her daughter Emma left for university, Sarah (whom we met at the beginning of this chapter) met her friend Diane for coffee again. This time, Sarah seemed different—more settled in herself.

"It hasn't been an easy year," she admitted. "There were days I barely recognised myself in the mirror. But I'm starting to see I didn't lose my identity when Emma left. I'm just expressing it differently now."

"What helped you get to that point?" Diane asked.

Sarah considered. "I started thinking about my life as a bridge—connecting who I've been with who I'm becoming. I'm not abandoning everything about my past, but I'm not stuck there either. I'm building connections between my experience as Emma's mum and what comes next."

The empty nest transition doesn't require building an entirely new identity from scratch. Instead, it invites you to construct the Identity Continuity Bridge—a structure honouring your parenting journey while creating a pathway to your next chapter.

This bridge is built on recognising that your identity was never just "parent" but always included the fundamental capability to architect meaningful transitions. Each element of the bridge connects aspects of your experience with future possibilities.

For Sarah, building her Identity Continuity Bridge meant recognising how the patience she'd developed helping Emma with homework could translate to teaching adult literacy volunteers. The organisational skills she'd honed managing family life now served her as event coordinator for community fundraisers. The emotional intelligence she'd cultivated, understanding her daughter's unstated needs, helped her connect with elderly neighbours who struggled to ask for assistance.

"I'm not just Emma's mum anymore," Sarah told Diane. "But I'm not a completely different person either. I'm bringing the best of what I learned and who I became during those years into what's next."

Your Identity Continuity Bridge has four essential components:

1. **Foundation: Your Core Capabilities.** Your abilities as a transition architect form the solid foundation. These capabilities have been expressed through parenting but exist independently of that specific role.

2. **Pillars: Your Values and Priorities.** What matters most to you will guide your choices, even as those choices take new forms in this next chapter.

3. **Spans: Your Transferable Skills.** The capabilities you've developed connect your experience to new applications, allowing your skills to extend into new domains.

4. **Destination: Your Evolving Vision.** Your developing vision for this next life chapter provides direction for the bridge, gaining clarity as you progress through the permission journey.

Building this bridge requires patience. You can't rush the process of identity evolution. But recognising that you're creating a bridge, not starting from scratch, makes the journey more manageable and honours the continuity of your core identity.

As we move into the next chapter, we'll explore how time, that suddenly abundant resource, creates challenges in the empty nest transition. You'll discover how to transform time from a source of anxiety to a canvas for your next chapter design. But remember: this transformation begins with recognising your fundamental identity as an architect of transitions, not just as a parent of children who have left home.

Your identity was never just a parent but always the architect of meaningful transitions. Embracing this truth creates the foundation for everything that follows.

Chapter 3

THE TIME WEALTH PARADOX

Janet stared at her phone calendar, her stomach tightening as she saw so much empty white space.

Three months earlier, when her youngest son had left for university, she'd imagined this moment countless times—finally having the freedom she'd craved for nearly two decades. No more rushing between soccer practices, helping with homework, or managing teenage crises. Yet now, faced with unscheduled hours stretching before her, Janet felt something unexpected: not relief, but a profound anxiety she couldn't explain to her friends who envied her "freedom."

"I spent years complaining about not having enough time," she confessed to her sister over coffee. "So why do I feel more overwhelmed now with nothing to do than I did when I had no time?"

Why Abundant Time Creates More Anxiety Than Scarcity
The Thursday morning group sat in a circle at the community centre, seven women and two men with one thing in common—all had become empty nesters within the past year. Elena, the group facilitator and an empty nester herself, wrote "The Time Wealth Paradox" on the whiteboard.

"Let me tell you about Michael," Elena began. "He's an executive who spent twenty years mastering time management while raising three kids. Colour-coded calendars, productivity apps, the works. Then his youngest left for college last fall."

She paused, making eye contact with each person in the circle.

"Within two months, Michael came to me feeling completely lost. 'I've got twenty extra hours a week,' he told me, 'and I'm getting less done than ever before.' His words struck a chord with me because I'd experienced the same thing."

Heads nodded around the circle. This paradox—feeling more overwhelmed with abundant time than scarce time—wasn't unique to Janet or Michael. It represented a psychological principle few empty nesters anticipated.

"When your calendar was packed with your children's activities," Elena explained, "you operated within what psychologists call 'beneficial constraints'—limitations that improve function rather than hinder it. Those constraints created three advantages you've now lost."

She wrote on the board:

1. **Clear priorities**: When time was scarce, decisions were simplified. Your child's needs took precedence, creating an automatic hierarchy for your attention and energy.
2. **Reduced decision fatigue**: With limited time slots, many choices were eliminated by default. You couldn't attend your book club if it conflicted with your daughter's recital, sparing you the mental toll of decision-making.
3. **Built-in purpose**: Each schedule item is connected directly to your core identity as a parent, giving even mundane tasks meaning within your primary life role.

"The sudden removal of these constraints leaves you facing what researchers call 'the paradox of choice'—the psychological burden that comes with too many options and insufficient guidelines for choosing between them," Elena continued.

A woman named Rachel raised her hand. "That explains why Sunday afternoons are the worst for me. I used to spend them preparing for the school week. Now they stretch out endlessly, and I do nothing at all."

The group murmured in agreement. This helped explain why many of them felt more overwhelmed with 20 extra hours per week than they did with none. Without the organisational framework children's schedules provided, they were suddenly responsible for managing time and determining what time was *for*.

"Let's do a quick self-assessment," Elena suggested, distributing a worksheet.

Time Anxiety Self-Assessment

Symptom	Rarely	Sometimes	Often
I feel guilty when I have unstructured time.			
I procrastinate on personal projects despite having time.			
I feel anxious when looking at my empty calendar.			
I fill time with busywork rather than meaningful activities.			
I feel less productive despite having more hours available.			
I struggle to start my day without external deadlines.			
I feel aimless or directionless with free time.			

As they completed the assessment, Elena reminded them: "The more 'often' responses you mark, the more you're experiencing the time wealth paradox. This isn't a character flaw—it's a natural response to a significant structural change in your life."

The Hidden Structure That Children's Schedules Provided

Sam, a former military officer and single father, spoke up when the group reconvened the following week. His transition to the empty nest had been challenging after raising two daughters alone for fifteen years.

"When you mentioned 'hidden structure' last session, something clicked for me," he said. "In the military, structure was explicit—clearly defined roles, responsibilities, and schedules. As a single dad, I created similar explicit structures for our household. But now I see there was an invisible structure my daughters' lives created that went far beyond our family calendar."

Elena nodded encouragingly. "Tell us more about that invisible structure, Sam."

"Monday was gymnastics night," he began, counting on his fingers. Tuesday was tutoring. Wednesday was family dinner. Thursday was swim practice. Friday was social time. Weekends were for tournaments and family activities."

His eyes grew distant with the memory. "This wasn't just a schedule—a complete life organisation system. It gave me built-in social connections with other parents. It reinforced my identity as a father every day. It gave me automatic purpose—contributing to my girls' development. It even set boundaries on my personal choices based on their needs."

Sam's voice cracked slightly. "That entire support structure vanished when they left for college last year. Suddenly, the simple question 'What should I do today?' required me to think about my purpose, identity, priorities, and values—previously handled implicitly through my role as their dad."

His story resonated deeply with the group. It explained why most felt lost than liberated by their newfound free time. The challenge wasn't merely filling hours but rebuilding an entire organisational structure for life.

"Sam's insight gives us an opportunity," Elena said, distributing another worksheet. "Let's identify the hidden structures in your children's schedules by completing this inventory."

The Hidden Structures Inventory

1. **Temporal anchors**: What weekly or seasonal events created predictable rhythms in your family schedule?
2. **Social connections**: Which relationships were maintained primarily through your children's activities?
3. **Purpose activities**: Which regular tasks gave you a clear sense of meaning through supporting your children?
4. **Decision simplifiers**: How did your children's needs help you Prioritise and make decisions about your time?

"Understanding what you've lost beyond just time commitments," Elena explained as they wrote, "is the first step toward intentionally designing new structures."

Time Intentionality Versus Time Reactivity

Olivia had developed a new morning ritual six months into her empty nest. Instead of immediately checking her phone for texts from her college-aged son or emails from work, she sat with her coffee and a small leather-bound journal. In it, she wrote three intentions for the day—not tasks or appointments, but how she wanted to direct her energy and attention.

It hadn't always been this way, and the first months after her son left had been chaotic. Though she had more time than ever before, she felt constantly behind and increasingly resentful of how her time seemed to slip away on other people's priorities.

"I realised I was still in 'mom emergency mode,'" Olivia shared with the group during their third session. "For eighteen years, I'd been trained to drop everything when my son needed something. That pattern didn't just disappear when he left for college—I was still in a constant state of readiness to respond to others."

Elena nodded, writing "Time Reactivity" on one side of the whiteboard and "Time Intentionality" on the other.

"Olivia has identified something crucial," she said. "During active parenting years, time reactivity serves a valuable purpose. Children's evolving needs demand flexibility and responsiveness—the ability to drop everything for a forgotten lunch, sudden illness, or emotional crisis. This reactive relationship with time becomes deeply ingrained, and for good reason: it's an effective strategy for the parenting phase of life."

She underlined "Time Intentionality" on the board. "But the empty nest requires a fundamental shift from time reactivity to intentionality. Let me show you the spectrum most of us move along during this transition."

She drew a table on the whiteboard:

The Time Orientation Spectrum

Time Reactivity	Time Intentionality
Responding to others' needs	Designing according to personal values
External deadlines drive action.	Internal purpose drives action.
Schedule determined by obligations	Schedule aligned with priorities
Time is something to be filled.	Time is something to be invested.
Requests determine direction	Direction is determined by vision.

"Most new empty nesters," Elena continued, "find themselves firmly on the left side of this spectrum, continuing to operate with time reactivity even when the external demands that made this approach necessary have diminished. This misalignment between approach and circumstance creates the feeling of being adrift."

Sarah, a former PTA president, raised her hand. "I think I see myself here. Since my twins left for college, I've somehow become the go-to person for every committee at church, my parents call with 'emergencies' daily, and my boss keeps adding to my workload because she knows I don't have kids at home anymore."

"That's what I call the 'perpetual responder' pattern," Elena said, writing it on the board. "You're continuing to organise time around others' requests and emergencies, now expanding beyond children to extended family, workplace, or community needs. This pattern keeps you in a reactive mode where time fills up with others' priorities rather than your own."

She added two more patterns:

"The 'habitual busyfiller' automatically packs schedules with activities to avoid the discomfort of unstructured time, often without evaluating whether these activities align with deeper values or desires. This creates the paradox of being simultaneously busy and unfulfilled."

"And the 'permission waiter' delays meaningful time investments until receiving external validation or invitation, often letting significant blocks of time pass while waiting for someone else to initiate or approve activities."

Several group members exchanged glances, recognising themselves in these descriptions.

"The shift to time intentionality," Elena explained, "begins with a critical question: 'What am I designing my time *for*?' This question transforms you from a responder to an architect."

To begin this transformation, she guided the group through an exercise:

Time Intention Setting Exercise

1. "If I were designing my time according to my deepest values, I would spend more time on..."
2. "The activities that make me lose track of time because I'm so engaged are ..."
3. "When I imagine myself at my most fulfilled, I spend my time..."
4. "The contributions I most want to make with my time are..."
5. "The relationships I want to invest more time in are..."

"These answers," Elena told them as they finished writing, "form the beginning of your time architecture blueprint—the foundation for intentional rather than reactive time allocation."

Becoming the Architect of Your Time

The fall leaves had turned to winter snow by the group's final session of the year. They gathered in the community centre, now decorated for the holidays, reflecting on their journeys since September.

Mia, a former school volunteer coordinator who rarely spoke in earlier sessions, shared her breakthrough.

"For months after my daughter left for college, I continued saying yes to everything—the hospital fundraiser, my sister's childcare emergencies, even helping my daughter with assignments she could handle herself." She paused. "When Elena asked why I wasn't pursuing my interest in painting, I remember saying 'it just feels selfish somehow.'"

Mia held up her phone, showing a photo of a half-finished canvas. "This is my first painting in twenty years. It's not very good," she laughed, "but starting it required something more difficult than artistic skill. It required permitting myself to use time for something that matters only to me."

Her story highlighted the critical link between the time-wealth paradox and the permission paradox explored in the previous chapter. The anxiety of abundant time wasn't just a practical scheduling challenge but a psychological challenge of authorisation.

"What Mia has demonstrated," Elena explained, "is that time architecture, like any skill, can be developed through practice. The GRANT Permission Escalation System that we'll explore in depth in Part II will provide specific tools to overcome the permission barriers that currently prevent many of you from truly acting as the architect of your time."

She looked around the circle at faces that showed more confidence than when they'd started three months earlier.

"For now, the most important step is simply recognising that your relationship with time needs to change fundamentally in this new life phase. Time reactivity—the orientation that served you well during active parenting—must gradually shift to time intentionality if you're to find fulfilment in your empty nest years."

Janet, who had shared her calendar anxiety in their first session, spoke up. "I've started blocking time in my calendar for things that matter to me—not just appointments with others, but with myself. It felt strange at first, but now those blocks of white space don't scare me anymore. They're opportunities to design rather than respond."

As winter light filtered through the community centre windows, the group members exchanged contact information and made plans to reconnect in the new year. They were still early in their empty nest journeys, but each had begun to see themselves differently, not just as former full-time parents, but as architects of their next chapter.

In Chapter 4, we'll explore how the 8-Week GRANT Permission Escalation System provides the progressive structure needed to overcome deeply ingrained guilt barriers and fully embrace the role of transition architect. This systematic approach builds upon your growing awareness of the time wealth paradox. It provides practical tools for transforming time anxiety into time architecture—the essential foundation for rebuilding identity and creating meaningful purpose in your empty nest years.

Chapter 4

Your Permission Breakthrough

The closing dormitory door echoed in Catherine's chest like thunder. September 2023 marked the day Catherine became an empty nester after dropping off her youngest at college. As she drove home alone, her mind acknowledged this new chapter should feel liberating, yet her body tensed with nameless dread when she considered what came next. Three months later, despite dozens of magazine articles about "finding yourself after kids," Catherine still spent evenings paralysed on the couch, mindlessly checking her phone for texts from her children while ignoring her neglected dreams.

Why Willpower Alone Fails to Overcome Permission Deficit
"Just do what makes you happy now!" Catherine's friend Diane insisted over coffee. "The kids are gone—nothing is stopping you!"

Catherine nodded, smiling weakly. She'd heard this advice countless times and given herself the same pep talk almost daily. Yet something invisible but powerful blocked her every attempt to move forward. Each morning, she'd wake with fresh determination to sign up for that photography class she'd postponed for eighteen years. Each day ended with the incomplete registration form, her camera gathering dust, and a growing personal failure.

"I kept telling myself to 'just do it,'" Sarah, a 52-year-old mother of two recently launched children, shared during a support group Catherine eventually joined. "Sign up for that class, say no to my daughter's requests to do her laundry when she visits, and spend money on myself without guilt. But something physically stops me. My heart races, my stomach tightens, and I find myself backing away from the edge. Then I feel worse for being 'too weak' to follow through."

Around the circle, heads nodded in silent recognition. The stories varied, but the pattern remained identical—intelligent, capable women paralysed between knowing they should move forward and unable to take even small steps toward personal fulfilment.

What these women didn't understand—what you might not Realise—is that their struggle wasn't about weakness. Research from the University of Pennsylvania reveals that willpower operates like a muscle that depletes with use. When you've spent decades overriding your needs to serve others, that muscle becomes specifically trained to resist self-prioritisation. Trying to overcome this through sheer determination is like attempting to lift a 300-pound weight after years of training specifically not to lift it.

This explains why traditional empty nest advice so often fails. Books and programs tell you what to do—find a hobby, reconnect with your spouse, explore new interests—but rarely address why executing these seemingly simple steps feels nearly impossible. The missing piece isn't information or motivation; it's permission.

The permission paradox works like this:
1. You intellectually understand you "should" prioritise yourself now
2. You attempt to act on this understanding
3. Deep emotional programming triggers physical and psychological resistance
4. You retreat from the discomfort
5. You blame yourself for lacking willpower
6. The cycle reinforces itself, deepening your sense of failure

Breaking this cycle requires understanding that different neural pathways govern intellectual knowledge versus emotional authorisation. Your brain has been rewired through years of parenting to prioritise others' needs. No amount of "trying harder" can override this programming without directly addressing the permission deficit.

The Psychological Foundation of Progressive Permission-Building
Jennifer stood frozen in her son's empty bedroom, dust cloth in hand, unable to move his soccer trophies to clean underneath them.

"I'm a clinical psychologist, for heaven's sake," she later admitted to her therapist. "I understood the empty nest concept intellectually—I even counselled other parents through it! But I found myself completely stuck. I couldn't even rearrange my son's bedroom without panic attacks."

What finally broke Jennifer's paralysis wasn't another self-help book or motivational speech. The breakthrough came unexpectedly, when she permitted an absurdly small action: moving one paperback book from his nightstand to the shelf.

"It sounds ridiculous now," Jennifer recalled, "but that tiny permission profoundly differed from my previous attempts to 'just get over it.' The next day, I permitted myself to move one shelf of books. Then, to create a reading corner while keeping his bed intact. Each small permission built on the last, and six weeks later, I'd transformed half the room into my writing space without a single panic attack."

Jennifer's story illustrates a fundamental truth about brain rewiring: incremental change succeeds where dramatic overhauls fail. Neuroscience research from Stanford University confirms that sustainable behaviour change occurs through progressive neural pathway strengthening. Each small permission you grant yourself creates a new path, and each repetition strengthens it.

This concept of permission-building rather than willpower-forcing represents a revolutionary shift for empty nesters. Consider these key differences:

Willpower Approach	Permission-Building Approach
Forces change through determination.	Creates change through progressive authorisation
Triggers resistance and discomfort	Works with your system rather than against it
Depletes with use	Strengthens with practice
Creates feelings of failure when unsuccessful	Builds confidence through small successes
Requires constant conscious effort	Gradually becomes automatic
Ignores emotional programming	Directly addresses emotional blocks.

The permission-building approach recognises that you deal with deep neural programming, not character flaws. After two decades of putting others first, your brain has developed powerful protective mechanisms around self-prioritisation. These can only be rewired through consistent, progressive permission experiences that gradually expand your comfort zone.

This explains why "cold turkey" attempts to transform your empty nest experience typically backfire. Whether redecorating your child's room immediately after they leave, booking an expensive solo vacation, or making dramatic career changes, these all-at-once approaches trigger maximum resistance from your permission-deficit system. The result isn't just failure but reinforced belief that change is impossible.

The Critical Difference Between Motivation and Authorisation

Rebecca stared at her hiking boots, still pristine in their box after six months, while her husband, Michael, headed out the door for another weekend adventure.

"What's wrong with me?" Rebecca asked during our first coaching session. "Michael wants me to join his new hiking group, and I want to go...but when Saturday morning comes, I find myself making excuses and staying home. I'm motivated but can't seem to follow through."

Michael and Rebecca had been married for 26 years and raised two children who had both recently left home. While Rebecca struggled with the empty nest transition, Michael seemed to adapt immediately, efficiently pursuing new hobbies and social connections.

Rebecca's situation perfectly illustrates the gap between motivation (wanting to change) and authorisation (believing you're allowed to change). She had plenty of motivation but lacked the critical emotional permission to act on it. This distinction explains why conventional advice fails so many empty nesters—focusing exclusively on building motivation while ignoring the authorisation deficit.

"What happened when you packed your hiking bag the night before?" I asked Rebecca.

She looked surprised. "How did you know I tried that?"

"Because you're not lacking motivation," I explained. "You're lacking permission."

Over the following sessions, Rebecca recounted how she'd tried every motivational strategy imaginable, setting out her clothes, watching inspiring hiking videos, even paying for an annual pass to the state parks. Yet when Saturday mornings arrived, she experienced an overwhelming physical sensation she described as "a wall of no" that prevented her from following through.

This wall wasn't laziness or lack of desire—it was the physical manifestation of permission deficit. Her emotional brain wouldn't authorise the action her intellectual brain knew she wanted to take.

Motivation vs. Authorisation: Key Differences

Motivation	Authorisation
Wanting to change	Believing you're allowed to change
"I should go hiking"	"I have permission to go hiking"
Comes from external advice and examples	Must come from within (self-authorisation)
Often already present in empty nesters	Frequently, the missing element
Can be increased through inspiration	Must be built through progressive practice
Operates in conscious awareness	Works at deeper emotional levels
Fluctuates based on mood and circumstances	Needs to become a stable foundation

This distinction has profound implications for your empty nest journey. Trying to overcome a permission deficit with more motivation is like trying to unlock a door by pushing harder—you're using the wrong tool for the job. No amount of wanting, wishing, or self-lecturing will open the door that can only be unlocked with permission.

Most empty nesters already have sufficient motivation. They want to find a new purpose, rebuild their identity, and create meaningful daily structures. What they lack is the emotional authorisation to act on these desires without triggering debilitating guilt, anxiety, or uncertainty. This explains why well-meaning spouses, friends, and even therapists often grow frustrated when their encouragement ("You should take that class!" "You deserve to travel!") fails to produce action.

How the 8-Week GRANT System Addresses Permission Deficit Paralysis

Maria's kitchen counter overflowed with care packages—carefully labelled boxes containing homemade cookies, vitamin supplements, and handwritten notes for her adult daughters who had moved away three years earlier.

"I know I need to move on," she explained during our first meeting, hands trembling as she described her daily routine that still revolved around checking in with her daughters multiple times daily, sending weekly packages, and keeping their rooms exactly as they left them. "But whenever I try, I feel physically ill with guilt. It's like I'm abandoning them, even though intellectually I know that's ridiculous."

Maria's experience represents permission deficit at its most extreme—where the gap between intellectual understanding and emotional authorisation creates complete paralysis. What finally worked for Maria wasn't more motivation or willpower but a structured permission-building system that progressively expanded her comfort zone.

Maria welcomed me into a transformed home six months after beginning the GRANT Permission Escalation System. The shrine-like bedrooms had become a guest room and art studio. The kitchen counter held a half-finished watercolour rather than care packages. And most tellingly, Maria's phone sat face down, unchecked for hours while we talked.

"I still love my daughters fiercely," Maria explained, "but I finally have permission to love myself too. The difference isn't that I care about them less—I finally believe I'm allowed to care about myself equally."

The GRANT Permission Escalation System works differently from conventional approaches because it addresses the root cause of empty nest paralysis. Rather than telling you what to do, it systematically builds your capability to permit yourself to do anything. This shift from specific actions to permission capacity creates lasting transformation rather than temporary change.

Each letter in GRANT represents a progressive stage in your permission journey:

G - **Ground:** Establish your permission foundation
R - **Reclaim:** Recover small daily permissions
A - **Amplify:** Expand permission to meaningful domains
N - **Normalise:** Integrate permission into daily thinking
T - **Transcend:** Move beyond permission to entitlement.

This carefully calibrated sequence addresses the permission deficit where it lives —in your emotional brain rather than your intellectual understanding. By starting with small, foundation-building permission exercises and progressively expanding to more challenging domains, the system creates success experiences that gradually rewire your neural pathways.

Consider how this worked for Catherine, whom we met at the beginning of this chapter. Her first permission was to spend fifteen minutes looking at photography websites without feeling guilty. This tiny authorisation triggered minimal resistance. The following week, she permitted herself to hold her camera again and take three photos of anything she wanted. Six weeks later, she had authorised herself to spend money on a photography class and block three hours weekly for this pursuit.

The GRANT system's recognition of the permission hierarchy makes it particularly effective for empty nesters. Some permissions trigger minimal resistance (spending 15 minutes reading without interruption), while others activate maximum guilt responses (redecorating a child's room, pursuing a long-postponed dream, setting boundaries with adult children). The system strategically builds your permission muscle through manageable challenges before tackling the high-resistance areas.

The 8-week timeframe provides another critical component: structure. After decades of having your time organised around children's schedules and needs, the formlessness of empty nest time often creates paralysing anxiety. The GRANT system offers a clear, time-bounded framework that replaces the missing external structure with intentional progress.

In the chapters ahead, you'll learn exactly how to implement each phase of the GRANT system in your own life. You'll discover specific permission exercises calibrated to your comfort level, language patterns that strengthen self-authorisation, and progressive practices that expand your permission capacity across all life domains.

Chapter 5

THE GRANT SYSTEM: YOUR PERMISSION ESCALATION FRAMEWORK

MARGARET stood frozen in the doorway of her daughter's empty bedroom, unable to cross the threshold.

For twenty-three years, she had defined herself through motherhood—scheduling her life around soccer practices, organising family meals, and staying up late to help with school projects. Three months after her youngest had left for college, Margaret was paralysed by a strange new freedom. Each morning brought the same crippling question: What am I allowed to do with my life now?

"I know it's ridiculous," she confessed to her sister over coffee. "I'm a grown woman with a successful career. Of course, I can do whatever I want. But every time I try to focus on myself, this overwhelming guilt stops me cold. It's like I need someone's permission—but whose?"

Margaret's experience reveals the hidden barrier that keeps countless empty nesters stuck in limbo: permission deficit.

The Psychology of Progressive Permission

Dr. Rachel Morgan still remembers the exact moment she identified the pattern. As a psychologist specialising in midlife transitions, she had worked with hundreds of empty nesters over fifteen years. Still, the breakthrough came during a session with a 52-year-old former PTA president named Sarah.

"I've tried everything," Sarah explained, frustration evident in her voice. "I signed up for that painting class I always wanted to take, but cancelled at the last minute. I planned a weekend away with my college friends, then made up an excuse about work. I keep sabotaging myself, and I don't understand why."

Dr. Morgan leaned forward. "Sarah, do you feel you have permission to do these things?"

The question hung in the air as Sarah's eyes widened with recognition. "Permission? I—I never thought about it that way. Who would even permit me?"

That conversation sparked years of research into what Dr. Morgan now calls "permission deficit disorder"—a condition particularly prevalent among empty nesters who have spent decades prioritising their children's needs above their own.

Brain scans conducted at Columbia University revealed the neurological basis for this phenomenon. When longtime caregivers attempted to prioritise themselves, their brains showed activity patterns remarkably similar to those of people violating deeply held moral codes. Essentially, their neural pathways had been wired to perceive self-focus as fundamentally wrong.

"What makes this so challenging," Dr. Morgan explains, "is that the barrier operates below conscious awareness. People intellectually understand they have every right to focus on themselves, yet their emotional systems rebel against the idea."

This explains why willpower alone fails to overcome the permission deficit. The solution required a systematic approach to gradually rewire those neural pathways through progressive exposure rather than demanding an impossible overnight transformation.

Jennifer's story illustrates how this plays out in real life. After 22 years of motherhood, she decided to write the novel she'd been postponing since her first pregnancy. "I cleared my entire summer schedule," she recalls with a rueful smile. "Set up a beautiful writing space, bought a new laptop, and told everyone about my plans. Three months later, I hadn't written a single word. Instead, I found myself deep-cleaning the house, volunteering for extra work projects, and calling my kids several times a day to 'check in.'"

Jennifer didn't lack motivation or discipline—she lacked the capacity for permission. Her brain couldn't sustain the perceived violation of prioritising a personal project over others' needs.

The breakthrough came when Jennifer's therapist suggested starting with just 15 minutes of writing each morning. "It seemed pathetically small," Jennifer admits. "But something about explicitly giving myself permission for those 15 minutes made it possible. After a few weeks, I extended it to 30 minutes, then an hour. Six months later, I had completed the first draft of my novel."

Jennifer's experience demonstrates the power of progressive permission development—the foundation of the GRANT system.

The GRANT Framework: Your Five-Step Permission Escalation System

The GRANT system emerged from thousands of clinical hours with empty nesters struggling to reclaim their lives after their children left home. This framework systematically builds permission capabilities through five progressive phases:

Phase	Focus	Timeframe	Key Outcome
Ground	Establishing your permission foundation	Week 1-2	Psychological safety for self-authorisation
Reclaim	Recovering small daily permissions	Week 2-3	Permission "muscle" development in low-resistance areas
Amplify	Expanding permission to meaningful domains	Week 4-5	Applying permission to identity exploration and relationships
Normalise	Integrating permission into daily thinking	Week 6-7	Transforming conscious effort into automatic habits
Transcend	Moving beyond permission to entitlement	Week 7-8	Shifting from needing permission to recognising inherent entitlement

Each phase builds directly on the previous one, creating a permission staircase rather than an impossible leap.

Consider Lisa's journey through the GRANT system. At 54, she devoted herself entirely to raising three children while maintaining her career as a high school English teacher. When her youngest left for college, Lisa found herself adrift.

"I had all these dreams," she remembers. "Taking a cooking class in Italy, redecorating the house, maybe even dating again after my divorce. But this paralysing guilt would stop me whenever I tried to act on them. I'd end up cleaning out another closet or offering to babysit my nieces instead."

Lisa's turning point came when she discovered the GRANT system. She began with the Ground phase, creating a Permission Inventory that acknowledged her parenting accomplishments while affirming her right to move forward. Each morning, she read her foundational permission statements aloud, feeling initially awkward but gradually more comfortable with the language of self-authorisation.

In the Reclaim phase, Lisa started with small, 15-minute blocks of uninterrupted reading time—an activity that triggered minimal guilt. She used specific permission language before beginning: "I give myself full permission to enjoy this reading time without interruption or guilt." Within two weeks, these brief sessions no longer triggered emotional resistance.

The Amplify phase brought more significant challenges as Lisa expanded her permission practice to domains that had defined her identity. She developed specific permission statements for exploring new interests and created boundary scripts for interactions with her adult children. She scheduled a half-day permission retreat focused entirely on her own needs.

"The Normalise phase was where everything shifted," Lisa recalls. "I created morning and evening permission rituals and placed visual triggers around my house. After a few weeks, I noticed I was automatically granting myself permission without the conscious effort it had required before."

By the Transcend phase, Lisa had moved beyond needing permission to recognising her inherent entitlement to self-prioritisation. She crafted a personal Declaration of Entitlement that now hangs framed in her home office. Eight weeks after beginning the GRANT system, she booked that cooking class in Italy, without a trace of the guilt that would have previously overwhelmed her.

"The best part wasn't even the trip itself," Lisa says, "but the fact that I planned it without a second thought. It felt like the most natural thing to prioritise my dream."

The Sequential Nature of Permission Development

Carlos learned the importance of this sequential approach the hard way. After 25 years of coaching his sons' baseball teams and building his identity around being "Coach Dad," he was utterly lost when his youngest left for college.

"I decided I was going to reinvent myself completely," Carlos explains. "I would lose 30 pounds, start a new business, and rebuild my social life all at once. I announced these plans to everyone, then proceeded to accomplish absolutely nothing. Each morning, I'd wake up paralysed by anxiety, unable to take even the first step toward these goals."

Carlos had attempted to skip directly to what would have been the Transcend phase, trying to leap from decades of self-sacrifice to complete self-prioritisation without building the necessary foundation. Like trying to lift a 300-pound weight without prior training, his permission muscles weren't developed enough for such a dramatic shift.

His breakthrough came when he scaled back to much smaller permission practices. "I started with permitting myself to watch a baseball game just for enjoyment, not as a scouting mission for coaching. Then I expanded to taking a 30-minute walk daily just for my health. Each small success built my confidence for the next step."

Six months later, Carlos had indeed lost 25 pounds, started a part-time consulting business, and rebuilt his social connections—not through a dramatic overnight transformation, but through progressive permission development.

This process works like strength training for your permission capacity. You begin with manageable resistance and gradually increase as your psychological muscles develop. Each phase of GRANT provides just enough challenge to build your permission capabilities without triggering the overwhelming guilt that derails progress.

How the Phases Work Together

The five phases of GRANT create a coherent journey from tentative permission-seeking to genuine entitlement:

Ground establishes your psychological foundation for self-authorisation. Diana, a 56-year-old empty nester, described this phase as "giving myself permission even to consider permission." Through her Permission Inventory, she acknowledged her successful parenting journey and her right to evolve beyond that primary role, creating the safety needed to begin the permission-building process.

Reclaim focuses on small, daily permissions with minimal resistance. Michael, a 62-year-old father of three, practised giving himself permission for a 20-minute coffee break each morning without checking his phone. "These small permissions were like training wheels," he explains. "They proved to my emotional system that prioritising myself wouldn't cause my world to collapse."

Amplify expands your permission practice to more meaningful domains. Having built basic permission capabilities, you can apply them to areas that significantly impact your next chapter. For Elena, a 48-year-old mother who had postponed her education for two decades, this meant permitting herself to research degree programs. This step would have triggered overwhelming guilt before developing her permission foundation.

Normalise transforms conscious permission-granting into automatic self-authorisation. Robert, a 58-year-old father who had defined himself through his children's achievements, created permission rituals and environmental triggers that gradually rewired his thought patterns. "After a few weeks, I noticed I was naturally thinking from a permission perspective rather than having to override my guilt consciously."

Transcend elevates you from needing permission to recognising your inherent entitlement to self-prioritisation. Sophia, a 51-year-old mother of twins, describes this phase as "the moment I realised I no longer needed to justify focusing on myself. It wasn't just permitted—it was my right."

Your 8-Week Journey: What to Expect

As Melissa approached her first empty nest weekend, the calendar was frighteningly blank after decades of soccer tournaments and dance recitals, and she felt terror and possibility in equal parts. The GRANT system provided a structure to navigate this uncharted territory.

During Weeks 1-2 (Ground), Melissa initially resisted even the concept of self-permission. "It felt selfish and indulgent," she remembers. "But I followed the exercises, creating my Permission Inventory and crafting permission statements. By the end of the second week, something shifted. I realised seeking permission wasn't selfish—it was necessary after decades of putting everyone else first."

In Weeks 2-3 (Reclaim), Melissa began practising small daily permissions—15 minutes of meditation each morning and permission to leave the dishes until morning. "My emotional responses fluctuated wildly," she recalls. "Some days I'd feel liberated, others overwhelmed with guilt. The Permission Journal helped me track these patterns and see gradual improvement."

Weeks 4-5 (Amplify) brought the first significant tests as Melissa expanded permission to more meaningful domains. "When I permitted myself to explore part-time work in interior design—my pre-children passion—my husband seemed threatened by the change. The boundary-setting tools helped me navigate his reaction without retreating to old patterns."

During Weeks 6-7 (Normalise), Melissa focused on making permission automatic. "I created a permission altar in my bedroom with visual reminders, and established morning and evening rituals that reinforced self-authorisation. One day, I realised I'd spontaneously signed up for a weekend workshop without the agonising deliberation it would have required before."

In Weeks 7-8 (Transcend), Melissa crafted her Declaration of Entitlement—a powerful statement of her inherent right to self-prioritisation. "Writing those words was emotional. I realised how long I'd been waiting for permission that could only come from myself. Reading my declaration aloud daily transformed how I approached my time and energy decisions."

Eight weeks later, Melissa's calendar was thoughtfully filled—not with obligations to others, but commitments to herself and her future. "The GRANT system didn't just give me tools for this transition," she reflects. "It fundamentally changed my relationship with myself."

Your journey through GRANT may follow a different timeline. Some people progress quickly through certain phases while needing more time with others. The weekly timeframes serve as guidelines rather than rigid requirements. Consistent practice is key—just as physical exercise requires regular repetition, permission development needs steady attention to create lasting change.

Chapter 6

GROUND: ESTABLISHING YOUR PERMISSION FOUNDATION

THE morning Sarah's youngest son left for university, she found herself alone in his bedroom, holding his childhood teddy bear.

"Who am I now?" she whispered to the empty room. Sarah had defined herself through her children's needs for twenty-two years—school runs, packed lunches, football matches, and teenage dramas. Now, at fifty-three, the silence of her home seemed to mock her purpose. When her therapist suggested keeping a journal to explore her feelings, the simple act of setting aside thirty minutes for herself triggered an unexpected wave of guilt.

"This feels selfish," she confided to her friend Melissa over coffee the following week. "I spent decades putting my children first. Taking time for myself feels... wrong somehow."

Melissa, whose children had left three years earlier, smiled with recognition. "I felt the same way. But here's what I discovered—and what changed everything for me: You've been granting yourself small permissions all along."

As their conversation unfolded, Sarah began to see what Melissa meant. Throughout her parenting years, she'd carved out small spaces for herself— reading novels after the children were asleep, taking the scenic route home from work to enjoy ten minutes of solitude, maintaining her Saturday morning coffee ritual with friends. These weren't grand rebellions but rather necessary acts of self-preservation that allowed her to be the mother she wanted to be.

These small permissions—already part of your life—form the building blocks of your empty nest foundation.

Permission isn't something you need to create from nothing—you need to recognise, strengthen, and expand. By identifying how you've already allowed yourself to prioritise your needs in small ways throughout your parenting journey, you establish proof that self-authorisation has always been part of your psychological makeup.

Your journey to freedom begins here, with the first foundational practice: creating your Permission Inventory.

The Permission Inventory: Recognising Your Foundation

"I want you to make a list," Dr. Chen instructed Jennifer during their third session after her twins left for college. "Write down every single way you've given yourself permission throughout your parenting years."

Jennifer laughed dismissively. "That'll be a short list. My kids always came first."

"Humour me," Dr. Chen replied with a knowing smile.

Jennifer returned with a stunned expression and three pages of examples two days later.

"I never realised," she said, her voice soft with wonder. "All those little things I did—keeping a drawer of books just for me, taking the long route to the grocery store for those extra minutes of quiet, insisting on my morning coffee ritual before anyone could ask me for anything—were all forms of permission."

Your Permission Inventory will be a comprehensive list of ways you've already granted yourself allowances, creating a powerful record of your self-authorisation patterns. Like Jennifer, you'll likely be surprised by how many examples you discover. This inventory serves several critical purposes:

1. **Proof of capability**: It demonstrates that you already possess the ability to grant yourself permission
2. **Pattern recognition**: It helps identify areas where self-permission comes more naturally
3. **Confidence building**: It creates evidence that counteracts your inner critic's claim that self-prioritisation is "selfish"
4. **Starting point identification**: It highlights low-resistance areas where you can begin expanding your permission practice

Creating Your Permission Inventory: Step-by-Step

Begin by setting aside 30 minutes of uninterrupted time—a permission for many of you. Find a comfortable spot with your notebook or Permission Journal and follow this sequence:

First, close your eyes and mentally walk through a typical day during your active parenting years. Notice moments when you claimed something for yourself, no matter how small.

Next, work through these permission categories systematically:

- **Time permissions**: Taking time to read, pursue hobbies, or rest
- **Boundary permissions**: Saying no to requests or limiting availability
- **Purchase permissions**: Buying items solely for your enjoyment
- **Health permissions**: Prioritising doctor appointments or exercise
- **Pleasure permissions**: Indulging in activities purely for enjoyment
- **Social permissions**: Maintaining friendships separate from family
- **Space permissions**: Creating physical areas in your home just for you

"I was shocked," Jennifer admitted when she completed her inventory. "I'd been telling myself I was completely selfless, but I had created small pockets of self-care all along. I identified 27 permissions—from the obvious ones like my morning coffee ritual to subtler ones like always taking the window seat on family road trips because I loved watching the scenery."

Permission Inventory Questions: Digging Deeper

If you're struggling to identify examples in your own life, consider these questions:

- What small pleasures did you maintain throughout your parenting years?
- When did you say "no" to someone to meet your needs?
- What boundaries did you establish with your children as they grew?
- What personal rituals or routines did you protect, even during busy periods?
- What spaces in your home were primarily for your use?

- What purchases did you make primarily for your enjoyment?

Michael, a recently retired father of two, initially struggled with this exercise. "I was completely devoted to my family," he explained. "But when I thought about it, I realised I'd always maintained my Sunday morning run, rain or shine. For eighteen years, those forty-five minutes were sacred. The family knew not to schedule anything during that time. It wasn't just about fitness; it was my mental reset button."

Remember, these permissions might seem insignificant, taking the long way home to enjoy a few minutes of peace, keeping a chocolate stash just for yourself, or insisting on five minutes alone after work before engaging with family demands. Their significance lies not in their size but in what they represent: your innate capacity for self-authorisation.

Your Permission Journal: Documenting the Journey

Elena stared at the beautiful journal her colleague had given her as a retirement gift six months earlier. It sat untouched on her nightstand, its leather cover gathering dust. After thirty years of teaching and raising three children simultaneously, she'd finally retired, just as her youngest left for college. The timing should have felt perfect. Instead, she felt adrift.

"I don't know what to write," she confessed during her weekly call with her sister. "For decades, I wrote lesson plans and kept track of the kids' activities. But writing about myself? I wouldn't even know where to begin."

"Start with permission," her sister suggested. "Each day, write down one thing you're giving yourself permission to do, feel, or be."

That simple suggestion changed everything for Elena. She opened the journal that evening and wrote her first entry: "Today, I give myself permission not to know what comes next." The relief was immediate and profound.

Your Permission Journal will become both witness and guide throughout this transformation journey. Unlike general journaling, this focused practice creates accountability, tracks progress, and generates evidence that counteracts deeply ingrained guilt patterns. Research shows that documenting a process dramatically increases follow-through and creates psychological safety for change.

Setting Up Your Permission Journal: A Sequential Approach

First, select a journal that feels special—one that symbolises the importance of this journey. Michael, a recently retired father of two, chose a leather-bound journal his daughter had given him years earlier, but he'd never used. "It seemed fitting," he explained, "to use a gift from my child to document the journey of rediscovering myself after parenting."

Next, create these specific sections in your journal:

1. **Permission Inventory**: Your growing list of identified self-permissions
2. **Permission Statements**: Your foundational declarations (we'll create these next)
3. **Daily Practice**: Records of permission exercises and emotional responses
4. **Permission Victories**: Celebrations of successful self-authorisation
5. **Permission Challenges**: Documentation of resistance and how you addressed it
6. **Permission Evidence**: Tangible proof that self-authorisation benefits everyone

Michael dedicated the first ten pages to his Permission Inventory, which grew from 12 initial examples to over 40 as he became more attuned to recognising his permission patterns. "It was like developing a new sense," he explained. "Once I started looking for these patterns, I saw them everywhere."

Your Daily Permission Practice: Building the Habit

Elena established her journal practice each evening before bed—just five minutes to reflect on her day through the lens of permission. She began each entry with the date and the simple phrase: "Today, I give myself permission to..." followed by her focus for that day.

Following Elena's example, create this simple table in your journal:

Date	Permission Focus	Emotional Response	What I Learned

This structured approach transforms vague intentions into concrete action. As Regina, a mother of four adult children, discovered, "Seeing the empty rows waiting to be filled created accountability. Even on hard days, I would grant myself at least one small permission to have something to write in my journal."

Three months into her practice, Elena flipped back through her journal entries. The progression startled her—from permitting herself "to rest" and "to leave dishes in the sink occasionally" to more significant permissions like "to apply for the art class I've always wanted to take" and "to rearrange the living room furniture without consulting anyone." Each small permission had built upon the previous ones, gradually expanding her sense of entitlement to shape her life.

Foundational Permission Statements: Your Declaration of Rights

David stood in his son's empty bedroom, the ache in his chest both familiar and strange. After dropping Marcus at university three weeks earlier, he'd thrown himself into work, staying late at the office and bringing projects home on weekends. But today, as he folded the last of his son's left-behind t-shirts, the truth hit him: he used work to avoid facing the emptiness.

"Who am I if I'm not Marcus and Emma's dad?" he whispered to the quiet room.

That evening, David shared his struggle in our support group for empty nesters.

"I feel like I need someone's permission to figure out who I am now," he admitted. "For twenty-three years, every decision was filtered through my role as a father. Now what?"

"You don't need someone else's permission," I told him. "You need to claim that authority for yourself."

Together, we worked on crafting what I call Foundational Permission Statements—personalised declarations that directly address our deepest permission barriers while acknowledging both our parenting accomplishments and our right to move forward. These aren't generic affirmations but rather powerful claims to the authority we've earned through our parenting journey.

Creating Your Foundation Three: The Structure of Self-Authorisation

First, you'll develop three foundational permission statements that address your most significant permission barriers. Each statement follows this robust structure:

1. Acknowledge a specific parenting accomplishment
2. Assert your right to Prioritise yourself
3. Connect this right to a meaningful value

Example Structure: "Because I have successfully *[parenting accomplishment]*, I now give myself full permission to *[self-prioritising action], which honours* my value of *[core value]*."

Let's see how this structure transformed David's thinking. After reflection, he crafted these statements:

David's Foundation Three:
- "Because I have successfully raised two independent adults who are thriving in their careers, I now give myself full permission to pursue my career change, which honours my value of continuous growth."
- "Because I have demonstrated unwavering support for my children's dreams for over twenty years, I now give myself full permission to prioritise my dreams with the same dedication, which honours my value of authentic living."
- "Because I have created a safe home environment that allowed my children to develop their identities, I now give myself full permission to rediscover and express my own identity, which honours my value of personal truth."

Two weeks after crafting these statements, David made a decision he'd been putting off for years: he enrolled in an evening architectural design course—a passion he'd abandoned when he became a father. "Reading my permission statements each morning changed something fundamental," he explained. "I stopped waiting for someone to tell me it was okay to Prioritise myself."

Maria, another member of our group, took a different approach with her statements:

Maria's Foundation Three:
- "Because I have successfully guided my children through countless challenges with patience and wisdom, I now give myself full permission to use that same patience and wisdom for my journey, which honours my value of self-compassion."

- "Because I have maintained a household that supported three unique individuals in pursuing their paths, I now give myself full permission to discover my path with the same enthusiasm, which honours my value of purpose-driven living."
- "Because I have demonstrated the importance of hard work and dedication to my children, I now give myself full permission to dedicate similar effort to my well-being, which honours my value of modelling healthy adulthood."

These statements provided Maria the foundation she needed to make a bold decision: selling the family home and moving to a coastal town she'd always loved—something she'd never considered while her children lived there.

Jennifer, whose children had left home eighteen months earlier, focused her statements on boundaries and self-development:

Jennifer's Foundation Three:
- "Because I have successfully created opportunities for my children to develop their talents, I now give myself full permission to develop them without guilt, which honours my value of lifelong learning."
- "Because I have maintained healthy boundaries that allowed my children to develop responsibility, I now give myself full permission to maintain boundaries that protect my own needs, which honours my value of mutual respect."
- "Because I have demonstrated unconditional love for my children through all their changes, I now give myself full permission to love myself through this transitional period, which honours my value of authentic acceptance."

Personalising Your Foundation Three: A Step-by-Step Approach

Now it's your turn. To create your own Foundation Three, follow this sequence:

First, identify your most significant parenting accomplishments. These might include:

- Raising independent, responsible adults
- Supporting your children through specific challenges
- Creating a loving, secure home environment

- Teaching important values or skills
- Maintaining family traditions or connections

Next, identify the areas where you feel most guilty prioritising yourself:

- Taking time for yourself
- Pursuing personal interests or dreams
- Making decisions without considering your adult children
- Changing family traditions or your home environment
- Investing in your future

Finally, identify your core values that connect both your parenting and your future:

- Growth and learning
- Authenticity
- Compassion
- Independence
- Creativity
- Connection

The Power of Permission Language: Words That Rewire Your Brain

"I felt silly at first," Jennifer admitted. "Reading these statements aloud in front of my bathroom mirror seemed like something from a self-help book I would have mocked before." She smiled. "But after two weeks, something shifted. The words began to feel true."

Notice the specific language in these statements: "I give myself full permission." This phrasing is intentional and powerful. Rather than saying "I should" or "I want to," the permission statement acknowledges your authority to authorise yourself.

Dr. Eleanor Richards, psychologist specialising in life transitions, explains: "The phrase 'I give myself permission' activates the executive function of the brain, creating new neural pathways that bypass the guilt response. When repeated regularly, these pathways become stronger than the guilt pathways established during years of prioritising others."

Display your Foundation Three somewhere you'll see daily—perhaps the first page of your Permission Journal, on your bathroom mirror, or as a lock screen on your phone. Read them aloud each morning and evening, allowing the words to sink in over time.

"Six months after creating my permission statements," David shared, "I was offered a part-time position at an architectural firm—something I never would have pursued. When my daughter called to congratulate me, she said something that brought tears to my eyes: 'Dad, I'm so proud of you for doing something just for you. You taught us to follow our dreams—it's time you followed yours.'"

From Foundation to Practice

Six months after beginning her permission practice, Elena hosted a dinner party for friends—something she hadn't done before her children left home. As she arranged flowers in the centre of her dining table—rearranged now according to her preference rather than family functionality—she realised something profound.

"I feel different," she told me during our next coaching session. "Not just because my children are gone, but because I've changed how I see myself. I'm not just their mother waiting for them to need me again. I'm Elena—a woman with desires, boundaries, and direction."

This transformation began with the three foundation practices we've explored in this chapter:

1. Her Permission Inventory identified her existing capacity for self-authorisation
2. Her Permission Journal created structure and accountability for her daily practice
3. Her Foundation Three provided powerful permission language that addressed her deepest barriers

Together, these practices established the psychological groundwork she needed to move forward with confidence rather than guilt.

"The most surprising thing," Elena reflected, "was that permitting myself didn't diminish my love for my children or my role as their mother. If anything, it enhanced our relationship. My daughter said she feels less worried about me now that she sees me creating my own life."

This foundation acknowledges your parenting accomplishments and inherent right to evolve beyond the active role. It validates your journey while creating the building blocks for your next chapter. Like building a house, we must establish solid ground before constructing the walls and roof. Your permission foundation provides that essential stability.

As David discovered after crafting his Foundation Three: "I realised I'd been waiting for someone—my wife, my children, my friends—to tell me it was okay to reinvent myself. But the only person who could truly grant that permission was me."

Chapter 7

RECLAIM: RECOVERING SMALL DAILY PERMISSIONS

Sarah stood frozen in her kitchen at 10:30 on a Tuesday morning, coffee growing cold in her hand.

This time slot had been filled with purpose for twenty years—preparing for a client meeting, rushing to volunteer at the school, or tackling the mountain of household tasks that kept her family functioning. Now, six months after her youngest left for college, she faced an ocean of unstructured time with no external demands to guide her choices. The freedom she had craved for years now paralysed her with uncertainty. Who was she allowed to be now? What did she have permission to do with this newfound time?

Sarah's story reflects the hidden challenge at the heart of the empty nest transition: after decades of putting others first, permitting yourself becomes difficult.

Identifying Low-Resistance Permission Activities
"I thought I'd feel immediately liberated when both kids were settled at college," Sarah confessed during our coaching session. "But instead, I found myself waiting for someone to tell me what I was allowed to do next. I had these grand ideas about writing a book or taking art classes, but I couldn't seem to get started on anything. The guilt was overwhelming whenever I tried."

Sarah's experience illustrates the common trap that derails many empty nesters. The impulse to compensate for years of deferred dreams often leads to setting ambitious goals that trigger maximum resistance. When these significant initiatives falter under ingrained guilt, the resulting disappointment reinforces the belief that change is impossible.

The solution lies not in lowering your ultimate aspirations but creating a strategic bridge between your current state and your desired future. Research in behavioural psychology confirms that sustainable habit change follows a precise sequence:

1. **Start with actions that trigger minimal psychological resistance**
2. **Build consistent evidence of capability through repetition**
3. **Gradually increase the challenge as confidence develops**
4. **Expand to more significant domains once the foundation is solid**

For Sarah, this meant identifying simple activities that required permission but wouldn't activate overwhelming guilt. During our work together, she created this list of possibilities:

Activity	Time Required	Guilt Level (1-10)	Joy Potential (1-10)
Reading fiction before sunset	15 minutes	3	8
Walking without multitasking	20 minutes	4	7
Enjoying coffee without checking the phone	10 minutes	2	6
Listening to music without doing chores	15 minutes	5	9
Taking the scenic route while driving	Variable	3	7

"The activities seemed so small they were almost silly," Sarah admitted. "But something unexpected happened when I started granting myself these tiny permissions. The small wins created momentum. Each time I successfully permitted these little things, it became slightly easier to do it again."

Your first step in reclaiming daily permissions is to create your permission inventory. What small activities would you enjoy that require minimal time commitment and cause limited guilt? Aim for options that take less than 20 minutes and rate below five on your personal guilt scale. Focus on activities that can be integrated into your routine rather than requiring major schedule adjustments.

Record your options using the Permission Starter Worksheet at the end of this chapter. From your list, select three activities to focus on during the following week. The most effective starting points typically are:

- Require 15 minutes or less
- Can be done daily or every other day
- Don't significantly impact others in your household
- Connect to something you genuinely enjoy

Remember: these small beginnings aren't your ultimate destination—they're strategic stepping stones that build your permission capability for bigger changes ahead.

Using Specific Permission Language Before Self-Care

Two weeks into her permission practice, Sarah called me, frustrated. "I'm doing the activities, but they still feel stolen—like I'm getting away with something I shouldn't. The guilt hasn't decreased as much as I expected."

When we explored her approach, I discovered the missing element: Sarah was doing the activities but skipping the crucial step of explicitly permitting herself beforehand. She was hoping the guilt would fade through repetition alone.

This highlights a fundamental aspect of rewiring deeply ingrained psychological patterns: our language shapes our emotional response. After decades of external authorisation, your brain has become conditioned to respond to specific permission cues. Without explicit permission language, activities continue to feel unauthorised, regardless of their size or importance.

Michael, a 55-year-old father who had launched three children over the previous five years, compared the process to his experience learning meditation: "My thoughts would race, and I'd try to focus on my breath without any specific technique. I made little progress for months. Then an instructor taught me to silently say 'breathing in' and 'breathing out' with each breath. That simple language pattern gave my mind something concrete to latch onto, and suddenly meditation clicked. Permission statements work the same way—they give my brain a clear signal that wasn't there before."

Your permission statements need specific components to signal your brain effectively:

The Anatomy of Effective Permission Statements:

Component	Purpose	Example
Self-acknowledgment	Establishes you as the authority	"I, Jennifer,"
Authorisation verb	Makes permission explicit	"Give myself full permission to"
Specific activity	Names the exact action	"Read this novel for twenty minutes"
Timing element	Creates clear boundaries	"Before starting household chores"
Value statement	Connects to deeper meaning	"Because my enjoyment matters"

When Sarah implemented this structured permission language, her experience transformed. "Speaking permission out loud felt awkward at first, but the difference was immediate. The formal language seemed to convince a deeper part of my brain that this was legitimate. The guilt didn't disappear completely, but it decreased significantly."

For maximum effectiveness:

1. **Speak your permission statements aloud,** when possible, as verbalisation activates different neural pathways than silent thought
2. **Maintain consistent wording** for repeated activities to strengthen the association
3. **Use your name** in self-acknowledgement to reinforce your authority
4. **Be specific about time boundaries** to create clear start/end parameters
5. **Connect to values** rather than justifying based on productivity or others' needs

Develop three complete permission statements for your selected activities using the template provided. Practice them daily until the language becomes comfortable and familiar. Pay attention to which phrasing feels most effective for you, as the psychological impact varies between individuals.

Documenting Emotional Responses to Build Evidence

"The most powerful moment came three weeks into my permission practice," Sarah shared during our follow-up session. "I was feeling discouraged, wondering if anything was changing. Then I looked back at my permission journal and saw the evidence in black and white. My guilt ratings had dropped from 8s and 9s to mostly 4s and 5s. The physical tension I'd documented—the tight chest and clenched jaw—had gradually faded to mild unease. Seeing that progression made it impossible to dismiss my progress."

Sarah's experience demonstrates why documentation is essential rather than optional in permission work. The changes in your emotional responses happen gradually, making them difficult to perceive without explicit tracking. When discouragement strikes—as it inevitably will—your documented evidence becomes a powerful counter to the voice of doubt.

Your Permission Journal functions as both a progress tracker and a psychological anchor. For each permission activity, record:

Daily Permission Journal Entry Format:
1. **Date and time**
2. **Permission statement used** (exact wording)
3. **Activity completed**
4. **Initial emotional response** (guilt rating 1-10)
5. **Physical sensations** experienced during the activity
6. **Thoughts that arose** (note recurring patterns)
7. **Emotional state after** completing the activity
8. **Unexpected outcomes or insights**

Lisa, a 49-year-old mother of twin boys who had left for college the previous year, discovered through her documentation practice that her guilt response followed a specific pattern: "The first five minutes of any self-permission activity triggered the strongest guilt, usually 7 or 8 on my scale. If I persisted through those initial minutes, the guilt typically dropped to a 3 or 4. Without tracking, I would have quit during those difficult first minutes, never discovering that relief was just around the corner."

Your documentation serves multiple purposes:

- It makes abstract emotional shifts concrete and visible
- It reveals patterns in your permission responses that might otherwise remain hidden

- It creates accountability to continue the practice consistently
- It provides evidence to counter self-doubt during challenging periods
- It offers data to inform your progression to more challenging permissions

Begin your documentation practice using the Permission Response Tracker provided at the end of this chapter. Commit to daily entries for at least four weeks, even if some days involve repeating the same activities. The consistency of recording becomes a reinforcing ritual that underscores the significance of your permission work.

Gradually Expanding Your Permission Comfort Zone

Six weeks into her permission practice, Sarah sent me an excited message: "I did something that would have been unthinkable when we started—I registered for a weekend photography workshop that means I'll be away from home for two full days. The amazing part wasn't just doing it, but how differently it felt. The guilt was present but manageable, more like background noise than a blaring alarm. I knew I could handle it because I'd built up to this moment step by step."

Sarah's breakthrough illustrates the power of systematic permission progression. Like physical training, permission work requires gradually increasing challenges to continue building capability. Attempt too much too soon, and you risk being overwhelmed; stay too long with easy permissions, and your growth stagnates.

Your "permission" comfort zone can expand along four key dimensions:

Permission Progression Dimensions:

- **Duration** - Increasing time spent in self-permission activities
    - Example progression: 15 minutes → 30 minutes → 1 hour → half-day → full day
- **Frequency** - Engaging in permission activities more often
    - Example progression: once weekly → twice weekly → every other day → daily → multiple times daily
- **Significance** - Choosing activities with greater personal meaning or impact

- Example progression: reading → hobby class → personal project → significant life change
- **Visibility** - Practising permission in increasingly public contexts
  - Example progression: alone at home → with supportive spouse → with friends → with adult children → in public settings

The most effective strategy involves focusing on one dimension at a time. For instance, if you've successfully granted yourself permission for 15 minutes of reading three times weekly, begin by increasing to 20 minutes (duration) before adding a fourth day (frequency).

Barbara, who participated in our empty nest support group, described her experience with the visibility dimension: "Private permissions felt safe—no one could judge or question me. The discomfort was intense when I started setting boundaries with my husband about my Thursday evening art class. I kept waiting for him to permit me or tell me I was being selfish. When he accepted it as reasonable, I realised how much of my limitation had been self-imposed. That visible boundary-setting changed everything."

Your Four-Week Permission Expansion Plan:
Week 1: Establish baseline with three consistent low-resistance activities. Week 2: Increase duration of one activity by 25-50%. Week 3: Add one additional day of frequency to your most vigorous physical activity. Week 4: Practice one permission activity with a trusted person present

Track your expansion using the Permission Progression Chart, noting the objective changes and your subjective experience of each increase. Look for patterns indicating which dimensions feel most challenging or liberating for you.

The seemingly small practices you're developing in this chapter create the foundation for the more substantial work ahead. Just as an athlete builds fundamental strength before attempting advanced techniques, you develop the psychological muscles needed for meaningful identity reconstruction.

As you continue strengthening your permission capabilities through these daily practices, you'll find yourself ready for the next phase of the GRANT process: amplifying your permission to more substantial life domains. The confidence and evidence you're building now through these small daily permissions will become the bridge to the larger transformations waiting in your empty nest journey.

Chapter 8

AMPLIFY: EXPANDING PERMISSION TO MEANINGFUL DOMAINS

Sarah stood at her kitchen window, watching raindrops trace lazy patterns down the glass. The house felt eerily quiet—a silence that startled her six months after her youngest left for college.

"I've been taking those small steps we discussed," she told me during our coaching session. "I've started reading before bed instead of folding laundry. I declined to chair the fundraiser at church." She smiled, but her eyes revealed uncertainty. "But something still feels... missing. Like I'm just dabbling around the edges of my life."

What Sarah was experiencing marked a crucial transition point in the empty nest journey. The small permissions—carving out 15 minutes for tea, saying no to minor obligations—are vital first steps. But they're simply the training wheels for the profound identity reconstruction that transforms your empty nest experience.

From Supporting Character to Lead Role: Your Permission Evolution
The Amplify stage is where your permission practice expands beyond daily conveniences into the domains that matter most: your fundamental identity, key relationships, and vision for the future. This expansion doesn't happen accidentally—it requires deliberate practice and specific tools.

Rachel, a high school guidance counsellor and mother of three, described reaching this stage like hitting a wall. "I'd gotten good at the little stuff—taking a yoga class, buying clothes without feeling guilty. But I completely froze when my husband suggested we sell our family home and travel for a year. The permission muscle I'd been building suddenly couldn't lift this heavier weight."

This reaction makes perfect sense when you understand the psychology behind permission deficit. You've spent decades training your brain to seek validation for minor choices—what to wear, when to rest, how to spend small pockets of time. Now you're asking that same brain to authorise fundamentally reimagining who you are and how you relate to those you love most.

That's precisely why the Amplify stage provides structured approaches to strengthen your permission capabilities in these weightier domains.

Crafting Your Identity Exploration Permission Language

Jennifer arrived at our workshop clutching a notebook filled with possibilities. After 22 years as a stay-at-home mom, she felt simultaneously excited and terrified by the open canvas of her future.

"I've always wondered about teaching," she admitted quietly. "But every time I think about pursuing it, this voice in my head says, 'Who do you think you are? You're too old to start something new.'"

That internal voice represents the permission barrier Jennifer needed to overcome—not just intellectually understanding that she could explore teaching, but also emotionally authorising herself. The tool that helped her break through? Precisely worded permission statements are explicitly designed for identity exploration.

Creating Your Identity Permission Statements

Effective identity permission statements contain three essential components:

1. **Direct self-authorisation** - "I give myself permission to…"

2. **Specific exploration domain** - Name the exact identity area you're authorising

3. **Release from judgment** - End with "…without guilt, fear, or self-judgment"

The table below shows how this formula works across different identity domains:

Identity Domain	Permission Statement Example
Career Exploration	"I allow myself to explore teaching as a second career, even if I'm older than typical new teachers, without guilt, fear, or self-judgment."

Creative Identity	"I give myself permission to identify as a photographer and invest in professional equipment, without guilt, fear, or self-judgment."
Physical Identity	"I allow myself to Prioritise becoming physically stronger through consistent training, without guilt, fear, or self-judgment."
Intellectual Identity	"I give myself permission to return to school for my degree, even though it will change family routines, without guilt, fear, or self-judgment."
Social Identity	"I allow myself to cultivate friendships based on my authentic interests, not just as someone's mother, without guilt, fear, or self-judgment."

For Jennifer, writing these statements felt uncomfortable at first. "It seemed so formal, almost silly," she shared. But when she read them aloud daily, something shifted. "The more I said the words, the more I started believing them. After two weeks, I researched teaching certification programs without that crushing guilt."

This progression from resistance to authorisation is precisely why the permission language must be explicit and practised consistently. The statements serve as a counter-narrative to the decades of conditioning prioritising others' needs above your own.

Moving from Words to Action

Permission statements alone, however, aren't enough. They must be paired with concrete action steps that allow you to experience these emerging identities, even in small ways.

When Michael, a former financial analyst who'd stepped back from his career to raise his children, reached this stage, he struggled to bridge the gap between permission language and actual exploration. "I could say 'I give myself permission to explore becoming a small business consultant' all day long, but taking actual steps felt paralysing."

The solution was creating a structured Identity Exploration Action Plan with three specific components:

1. **Information Gathering** - Michael committed to reading three books on consulting and interviewing two people in the field
2. **Low-Risk Experimentation** - He offered to help a friend analyse their small business finances for free
3. **Reflection Process** - After each exploration activity, he documented his emotional response and energy level

"The small experiment was the game-changer," Michael explained six months later. "When I sat with my friend and looked at his business numbers, I felt this rush of confidence and purpose I hadn't experienced in years. That feeling gave me the courage to take bigger steps."

Your action plan should follow this same progression—gathering information, experimenting with low-risk activities, and carefully documenting your responses. This evidence-based approach builds confidence through direct experience rather than abstract consideration.

Setting Boundaries That Protect Your Emerging Self

Three months into her empty nest journey, Elena faced an unexpected obstacle—her adult children's resistance to her changing role.

"My daughter called, upset that I wasn't available to babysit my grandson on short notice," Elena explained, tears welling in her eyes. "She said, 'Mom, what's happened to you? You used to always be there when we needed you.'"

This reaction is painfully familiar as you expand your permissions into relationship domains. The people in your life have grown accustomed to your self-sacrificing patterns—they've built their expectations around your unlimited availability and accommodation. When you begin changing these patterns, their discomfort often manifests as criticism or guilt-inducing comments.

That's why boundary statements are an essential companion to expanded permissions. They directly address shifting relationship dynamics while creating protected space for identity exploration.

The Four-Part Boundary Formula

Effective boundary statements include four key elements:

1. **Pattern recognition** - Acknowledge the established dynamic
2. **Change declaration** - Clearly state what's changing
3. **New expectation** - Explain what you need going forward
4. **Relationship affirmation** - Express continued care (when appropriate)

Elena practised this formula until she could deliver her boundary statement calmly:

"I've always been available whenever you've needed childcare, and that's changing now. I need at least three days' notice to babysit from now on, except in true emergencies. I love you and adore my grandson; this boundary helps me be fully present with him."

The first time she delivered this statement, her daughter reacted with surprise and some defensiveness. However, their relationship adapted as Elena maintained her boundaries consistently over time. Six months later, Elena reported a profound shift: "My daughter apologised yesterday for assuming I'd always rearrange my plans for babysitting. She said she's proud of me for developing my own life."

This evolution represents the powerful ripple effect of boundary-setting. By clearly communicating your changing needs, you create space for your growth and model healthy self-care for those around you.

The table below provides examples of boundary statements for various relationships:

Relationship	Boundary Statement Example
Adult Child	"I know I've always been the one to initiate our phone calls and visits, and that's changing now. I'm expecting a more balanced initiation of our connection going forward. Our relationship remains significant to me."
Spouse	"I've noticed I automatically handle all holiday planning and family gifts, and that's changing now. I'll be sharing these responsibilities so I can pursue my art classes. Your partnership in this transition matters greatly to me."
Friend	"I've been the one who adapts my schedule to accommodate yours, and that's changing now. I need us to find times that work equally well for us. I value our friendship and want it to continue more balanced."
Parent	"I've been calling daily and managing your appointments without discussion, and that's changing now. I'll call thrice weekly and need you to maintain your calendar when possible. Your independence and my support can coexist."
Volunteer Group	"I've taken on last-minute projects whenever asked, and that's changing now. I'll only commit to tasks that align with my schedule and interests. I support this organisation and want to contribute in sustainable ways."

As you craft your boundary statements, remember that delivery matters as much as content. Practice speaking these statements aloud until you can deliver them calmly and without apology. Your tone should convey confidence in establishing these parameters, not uncertainty seeking approval.

The Permission Immersion: Your Half-Day Retreat

Lisa arrived at her cabin rental with a mixture of excitement and guilt. She'd never taken time away from her family solely for her needs—not for a spa day or girls' weekend, but specifically to focus on her permission practice.

"I felt ridiculous explaining it to my husband," she admitted. "Taking half a day just to... permit myself? It seemed so self-indulgent."

Yet this "self-indulgent" experience proved transformative for Lisa, as it has for countless empty nesters in my program. The half-day permission retreat is a psychological milestone, clearly stating that your needs deserve significant time and attention.

Unlike conventional self-care, which often revolves around temporary relaxation, this retreat focuses on strengthening your permission capabilities around life-changing domains. It's not about escaping your reality but about intentionally reshaping it.

Designing Your Permission Retreat

Your retreat should include six essential elements, each serving a specific purpose in your permission expansion:

1. **Opening Permission Ceremony (15 minutes)**

Lisa began her retreat by arranging photographs of herself at different life stages in a circle. In the centre, she placed a candle representing her future self. As she lit the candle, she read aloud: "I, Lisa Mitchell, give myself full permission to discover who I am beyond motherhood, to pursue interests that light me up, and to create boundaries that honour my needs—all without guilt, fear, or self-judgment."

This opening ritual serves as a powerful psychological anchor, setting both your intention and the emotional tone for the experience.

2. **Identity Exploration Activity (90 minutes)**

For this segment, immerse yourself in a meaningful activity that explores a potential new identity. Lisa had always been drawn to writing, but had set aside this interest when her children were born. During her retreat, she completed the first three exercises in a creative writing workbook, produced two short poems, and researched local writing groups.

"I was shocked by how quickly I lost track of time," she recalled. "After about twenty minutes, something shifted. I stopped thinking about what must be done at home and became completely absorbed in the words. I hadn't experienced that feeling of flow in years."

This immersive activity provides direct evidence of your capacity for engagement beyond your parenting role—crucial data for your permission-building process.

3. Reflection Process (45 minutes)

Following the exploration activity, document your emotional and physical responses in detail. Lisa noticed tension in her shoulders whenever she imagined sharing her writing with others. She wrote about the limiting belief behind this tension: "If I take my writing seriously, I'm being selfish and pretentious."

Then came the critical step—countering this belief with a permission statement: "I give myself permission to take my creative expression seriously, to share it with others, and to develop my voice as a writer, without guilt, fear, or self-judgment."

This reflection process identifies and directly addresses the specific permission barriers that arise when you engage more deeply with potential identities.

4. Physical Boundary Practice (60 minutes)

The retreat should include a physical representation of your evolving boundaries. Lisa chose to walk the perimeter of the cabin property, stopping at each corner to state a boundary she needed to establish:

"This is where I stop answering work emails after 6 PM." "This is where I decline volunteer requests that don't align with my priorities." "This is where I ask my husband to share household management equally." "This is where I stop automatically rearranging my schedule for adult children's requests."

The physical movement creates a powerful embodied experience of defining and defending your literal and metaphorical territory.

5. Forward Vision Exercise (45 minutes)

For this component, create a detailed description of your life six months in the future, after these amplified permissions have taken root. Lisa wrote a first-person account of a typical Thursday, describing how she started her morning with writing time, maintained clear work boundaries, and participated in an evening writing group without guilt or apology.

"As I wrote about this hypothetical day," Lisa shared, "it didn't feel hypothetical. It felt completely possible—a matter of consistent permission and boundary practice."

This forward-casting exercise bridges the gap between current permissions and future identity, making abstract possibilities tangible and achievable.

6. Closing Integration (30 minutes)

Conclude your retreat by reviewing key insights and identifying specific permission statements that feel stronger after this experience. Lisa realised her permission to pursue creative expression had strengthened significantly, while her permission to establish work boundaries still needed reinforcement.

Before leaving her retreat space, she scheduled her next permission retreat three months later, creating a concrete commitment to continued practice.

When Lisa returned home, her family noticed an immediate difference. "My husband said I seemed more centred, more decisive," she recalled. "And I felt I was finally taking the driver's seat in my life."

Taking Your Permission Practice Public

Two weeks after her retreat, Lisa faced an unexpected test of her expanding permission capabilities. At a neighbourhood gathering, someone asked, "So what do you do now that your kids are gone?"

In the past, Lisa would have deflected with a self-deprecating joke about being "just a mom looking for a purpose." But this time, drawing on her amplified permissions, she responded differently:

"I'm exploring my identity as a writer and looking into teaching writing workshops for women in transition."

The moment carried both vulnerability and power. By publicly declaring her emerging identity, Lisa amplified her self-permission in the most challenging context—social situations where her primary identity had always been "mom."

This type of public permission practice is essential to solidifying your expanded self-authorisation. Consider these three public exercises:

1. **The Public Identity Declaration.** When asked about yourself, respond with your emerging identity rather than defaulting to your parenting role. Use confident language even if the identity is still developing.

2. **The Preference Expression** In group settings, clearly state your preferences for activities, restaurants, or entertainment without first checking what others want or automatically deferring.
3. **The Time Boundary Assertion** When invited to events or asked for commitments, practice responding with "I'll need to check my schedule" rather than immediately accommodating others' timelines.

Each of these exercises strengthens your perceptual muscles in increasingly challenging contexts. The more you practice public self-authorisation, the more natural it becomes to prioritise your needs across all domains of life.

From Amplification to Daily Habits

As the rain subsided outside her kitchen window, Sarah turned to face me on our video call. "I think I understand now," she said thoughtfully. "These bigger permissions—exploring a new career, changing my relationship patterns, investing significant time in my interests—are not just nice additions to my life. They're the foundation for who I'm becoming."

Her insight captures the essence of the Amplify stage. By expanding your permission capabilities into meaningful domains, you're not simply adding pleasant activities to your schedule—you're creating the essential psychological space needed for profound identity reconstruction.

You've now developed specific permission language for identity exploration, created boundary statements for key relationships, designed your half-day permission retreat, and begun Practising permissions in public settings. These amplified permissions create the foundation for rebuilding your identity beyond your parenting role.

In the next chapter, we'll focus on the Normalise stage of the GRANT framework—transforming these conscious permission practices into automatic habits that shape your daily thinking and actions. You'll learn to establish permission rituals, create environmental triggers, and develop rapid response techniques that make self-authorisation your default operating system rather than a deliberate effort.

The path from conscious permission to automatic entitlement represents the final bridge between your past identity as a supporting character and your future as the author of your own story.

Chapter 9

NORMALISE: INTEGRATING PERMISSION INTO DAILY THINKING

SARAH stared at the blank canvas, paintbrush in hand, frozen by an invisible force.

Three months after her youngest had left for college, she'd finally cleared the corner of her bedroom for a painting space—something she'd dreamed about for years. She'd purchased supplies, set up an easel, and scheduled two hours for herself this Tuesday morning. Yet here she stood, unable to make the first stroke, her mind flooded with thoughts of the unfolded laundry downstairs, unanswered texts from her daughter, and the nagging sense that she was being selfish. "Why is this still so hard?" she wondered, setting down the brush with a sigh. "I know I deserve this time, so why can't I just take it?"

Sarah's struggle illustrates the crucial difference between intellectually understanding your right to self-prioritisation and emotionally feeling entitled to it. This gap explains why many empty nesters cannot enjoy the freedom they've intellectually claimed.

The Permission-Habit Connection

"I'll start taking ceramics classes when the kids are grown." "Once they're in college, I'll finally have time for myself." "When the nest is empty, I can focus on what I want."

How many variations of these promises did you make to yourself over the years? Yet now that this time has arrived, you've discovered that knowing you deserve permission and feeling entitled to take it are entirely different experiences.

The reason is neurological. Your brain has spent decades building neural pathways that automatically Prioritise others' needs before your own. These pathways are like well-worn trails through a forest—the path of least resistance, your thoughts naturally follow. Each time you set aside your needs for your children, you deepened these grooves, creating automatic patterns that now operate below your conscious awareness.

This is why the previous "Amplify" phase, while essential, isn't sufficient on its own. Conscious permission-granting is like hacking through underbrush to create a new path—it requires constant effort and attention. Without making this new path automatic, you'll inevitably revert to old patterns when you're tired, stressed, or emotionally vulnerable.

Karen, a 55-year-old former school volunteer coordinator and mother of two, described this phenomenon perfectly: "I'd write in my journal each morning that I deserved time to reread novels. I'd feel completely convinced. Then my son would call about his roommate troubles, and two hours later, I'd Realise I'd abandoned my reading plans without a second thought. It wasn't a conscious decision—it just happened."

This chapter transforms your conscious permission-granting into automatic self-authorisation through three powerful tools: permission rituals, environmental triggers, and rapid response techniques. By implementing these practices consistently over the next two weeks, you'll rewire your neural pathways until self-permission becomes your default setting rather than something you struggle to achieve.

Morning Permission Ritual: Setting Your Day's Foundation

The alarm chimed softly as Ellen reached to silence it. Before she could fall into her old habit of immediately checking her phone for messages from her children, she paused. Sitting in bed, she placed her hand over her heart and said, "I permit myself to Prioritise my needs today. My children are capable adults leading their own lives. I claim today to be my design as I choose."

After repeating these words, she reached for the small card on her nightstand and wrote down one self-care activity she committed to enjoying today. Only then did she pick up her phone, not with anxiety about what crisis might need her attention, but with the calm certainty that whatever messages awaited, her self-commitment remained valid.

Ellen's morning permission ritual illustrates how you can establish self-authorisation as your day's foundation. The early morning is neurologically significant—your brain is most receptive to new patterns immediately after waking, before the day's demands create stress and resistance.

Your morning permission ritual needs three specific elements to be effective:

- **Verbal Permission Declaration:** Speaking aloud is critical—your brain processes information differently when you hear it in your voice. Create three permission statements that address:
    - Your right to self-prioritisation
    - Release from constant caregiving obligations
    - Specific time claims for personal activities

- **Physical Permission Anchor:** Pair your verbal declaration with a physical gesture that engages your body in the permission process. This creates a somatic memory that deepens neural connections. Effective anchors include:
    - Hand over heart
    - Arms extended in an expansive posture
    - A gentle self-embrace

- **Written Permission Commitment:** Document at least one specific self-care activity you'll engage in today, using explicit permission language: "I give myself permission to..."

The power of this ritual lies in its consistency. A 2-minute ritual performed faithfully every morning creates stronger neural rewiring than a 20-minute practice done sporadically. Set your alarm 5 minutes earlier, if necessary, but never skip this foundation-setting practice.

Your Morning Permission Ritual Worksheet

Element	Template	Your Personalised Version
Permission Statement 1	"I grant myself permission to Prioritise my needs today."	[Create your statement]

Permission Statement 2	"My children are capable adults leading their own lives."	[Create your statement]
Permission Statement 3	"I claim today to be my design as I choose."	[Create your statement]
Physical Anchor	Hand over heart	[Choose your anchor gesture]
Today's Permission Activity	"I give myself permission to spend 30 minutes reading for pleasure."	[Write today's commitment]

Complete this worksheet now, then transfer your personalised elements to a notecard at your bedside. Tomorrow morning, begin your permission journey with this ritual before any other activity.

Evening Permission Reflection: Closing the Loop

Robert sat in his favourite chair; "Permission" Journal open on his lap. The house was quiet—a silence that once felt empty but now held possibility. He reflected on the day's permission moments, writing:

"Today, I permitted myself to decline helping my daughter move furniture in her apartment because I had tickets to the jazz concert I've been anticipating for months. When I told her I wasn't available, I felt a wave of guilt, but recognised it as my old pattern, not a signal I was making a wrong choice. I reminded myself that purchasing concert tickets was a valid use of my time and money. By the second song, I felt fully present and grateful for the experience rather than worried about my daughter's reaction. She found another friend to help and texted that everything worked fine."

Robert's evening reflection demonstrates how to close your day's permission loop, reinforcing new neural pathways and preparing your subconscious mind to continue permission-building during sleep. Research shows that the brain consolidates new learning during sleep, making your pre-sleep mental state particularly important for habit formation.

Your evening permission ritual should include:

- **Permission Success Documentation**: Record at least three moments you permitted yourself today. Include:
  - The specific permission you granted
  - Any resistance you felt

- How did you overcome that resistance
- The positive outcome of your self-authorisation

- **Permission Challenge Identification**: Note any situations where you struggled with self-permission, analysing them without judgment using these questions:
  - What triggered my permission hesitation?
  - What old pattern was I reverting to?
  - What permission statement would have helped in that moment?
- **Tomorrow's Permission Intention**: Set a specific permission intention for tomorrow, identifying one area where you'll practice stronger self-authorisation.

This evening practice takes only 5-10 minutes but dramatically accelerates your permission normalisation by creating conscious awareness of progress and challenges. Keep your Permission Journal beside your bed with a pen ready, making this reflection the last activity before sleep.

Permission Success Template

For each permission success, complete this framework in your journal:

"Today I permitted myself to [specific activity]. When I [describe the situation], I felt [emotional response] but recognised it as [old pattern or new understanding]. I reminded myself of the [permission statement]. Afterwards, I felt [positive outcome]."

By bookending your day with these morning and evening rituals, you create a permission container for everything between them. Over time, this container becomes internalised, transforming permission from a deliberate practice into your default psychological setting.

Creating Environmental Permission Triggers

Jennifer entered her kitchen, automatically glancing at the refrigerator where a new magnet caught her eye: "Your needs matter too." She smiled, reaching for her favourite mug with "Permission Granted" printed on the side, which she used exclusively for her morning coffee ritual. While waiting for the water to boil, she noticed the small easel on the counter displaying today's permission card: "I am entitled to pursue my interests without apology."

These weren't random decorations. Jennifer had strategically created environmental permission triggers throughout her home, visual cues that prompted automatic self-authorisation thoughts dozens of times daily without requiring conscious effort.

Your physical environment either reinforces or undermines your permission journey. Most empty nesters live surrounded by reminders of their parenting role—children's photos dominating wall space, household systems designed around family needs, spaces arranged for others' comfort rather than personal preferences.

Environmental permission triggers work by intercepting your automatic thought patterns with visual cues that prompt new, permission-based thinking. Each time you encounter these triggers, your brain receives a micro-dose of permission reinforcement, gradually changing your default settings.

High-Impact Environmental Triggers

Location	Trigger Type	Example	Permission Message
Bathroom mirror	Visual affirmation	Decorative frame with permission statement	"I authorise myself to design my life around my priorities."
Refrigerator	Decision reminder	Magnet with an entitlement phrase	"My needs matter too."
Front door	Boundary reinforcement	Small plaque with permission statement	"I choose how I spend my time and energy."
Bedside table	Identity reminder	Object representing non-parent identity	Art supplies, travel books, or professional symbols
Phone lockscreen	Digital reminder	Permission wallpaper	Image with "Permission Granted" text overlay

Michael, a 59-year-old father who had always managed the family calendar, created a powerful environmental trigger by replacing the family scheduling board with a beautiful new calendar solely for his activities. "Every time I walk past it, I'm reminded that my time belongs to me now," he explained. "The first week felt strange, almost wrong. By the third week, I automatically planned activities I enjoyed without the guilt that used to paralyse me."

When creating your environmental triggers, focus on locations you encounter multiple times daily during automatic routines—brushing teeth, preparing meals, entering or leaving your home. The power lies not in the trigger's size or cost but in its consistent presence in your daily path.

This week, create at least three environmental permission triggers and place them strategically in your home. Pay attention to your emotional response when you first encounter them—any discomfort signals you're challenging established neural patterns, precisely the productive disruption needed for change.

Developing Rapid Permission Responses

The phone rang just as Lisa settled into her newly established writing nook. Glancing at the caller ID, she saw it was her daughter, likely calling about wedding planning details. Her hand moved automatically to answer, but then she paused, taking a deep breath. "I can respond without reacting," she reminded herself. Instead of immediately answering, she sent a quick text: "In the middle of my writing time. Can I call you at 11?" Then she silenced her phone and returned to her notebook, the momentary guilt fading as she reconnected with her story.

Lisa's response demonstrates the power of prepared permission scripts that allow you to maintain boundaries when unexpected situations arise. Without these rapid responses, many empty nesters find their permission muscles collapse in the moment, reverting to ingrained caregiving responses before conscious choice can intervene.

Rapid permission responses are pre-prepared scripts for high-challenge situations that you can deploy immediately, bypassing the guilt-induced paralysis that often occurs in emotional moments. By developing these scripts now and practising them regularly, you'll build the mental muscle memory to maintain your permission boundaries even when caught off-guard.

Essential Rapid Response Categories

- **Time Boundary Scripts**: For unexpected requests that threaten your planned self-care time
    - Internal reminder: "My time has value. I can respond without immediately reacting."
    - Verbal response: "I've committed this time to myself. Can we connect at [alternative time]?"

- Digital response: "I'm in the middle of [personal activity]. I'll be available after [time]."

- **Emotional Support Limits**: For adult children seeking excessive emotional support
    - Internal reminder: "I can offer wisdom without taking responsibility for their feelings."
    - Verbal response: "That sounds challenging. What options are you considering?"
    - Follow-up: "I trust your ability to handle this situation."

- **Guilt Deflection Statements**: For when others imply selfishness in your self-care
    - Internal reminder: "Their perspective doesn't define my entitlement."
    - Verbal response: "After [X] years of prioritising others, I'm creating balance in my life now."
    - Self-reinforcement: "My self-care enables me to be fully present when I engage."

- **Internal Critics Counter**: For when your guilt voice activates
    - Recognition: "This is my permission deficit voice, not my truth."
    - Counter-statement: "I've earned the right to Prioritise myself."
    - Action: Immediately engage in a small permission action to reinforce your entitlement.

David, a 61-year-old father whose identity had been wrapped up in being the family problem-solver, developed a rapid response for crisis calls: "I'm here to listen and offer perspective, but you're capable of handling this." Using this script for the first time, his son called about a work conflict that felt almost physically painful. "Everything in me wanted to jump in and fix it," he shared. "But I stuck to my script, and not only did my son figure it out himself, but he also thanked me later for not taking over."

This week, identify your three highest-risk permission challenges—the specific situations where your permission resolve is most likely to crumble. Create personalised rapid responses for each using the categories above. Write these scripts on small cards in your wallet, purse, or phone case for immediate access when challenges arise.

Practice your responses daily, speaking them aloud when alone. Your brain must repeatedly hear these words in your voice to accept them as valid responses. The goal is to make these scripts so familiar that they become your automatic reaction in high-pressure moments.

From Conscious Effort to Automatic Habit
Six weeks into her permission journey, Teresa noticed something surprising while shopping. As she picked up a book she wanted to read, there was no internal debate about whether she deserved to spend money on herself. She placed it in her cart alongside groceries, recognising it as an equally valid purchase. It wasn't until she was driving home that she realised the significance: permission had become automatic rather than something she had to grant herself consciously.

This shift from deliberate permission to automatic entitlement marks the successful completion of the normalisation phase. Psychological research shows that habit formation typically requires around 66 days of consistent practice, so our 8-week program provides sufficient repetition for actual neural rewiring.

You're creating new default settings in your brain by consistently implementing the rituals, environmental triggers, and rapid responses outlined in this chapter. Rather than permission being something you struggle to achieve, it becomes your automatic operating system.

Signs that permission is becoming normalised include:

- Making self-priority decisions without internal debate
- Noticing decreased emotional resistance to self-care activities
- Feeling discomfort when you don't honour your needs
- Automatically using permission language without reminders
- Responding to boundary violations with immediate permission assertions

If you're not experiencing these shifts, increase the frequency of your permission rituals and environmental triggers. Some participants benefit from hourly permission reminders on their phones until the habit solidifies. The key is consistency—neural rewiring requires repetition more than intensity.

As we close this normalisation phase, you're standing at the threshold of your permission journey's final, most powerful stage: transcendence to entitlement. When permission becomes automatic, you're ready to move beyond permitting yourself to recognising your inherent right to self-prioritisation.

In our next chapter, "Transcend: Moving Beyond Permission to Entitlement," you'll craft your personal Declaration of Entitlement, develop powerful visualisation practices, and learn to maintain your entitlement even when facing resistance. This final step will transform your relationship with yourself from someone who occasionally deserves permission to someone who is fundamentally entitled to design your life around your priorities—the ultimate shift from supporting character to author of your own story.

Chapter 10

TRANSCEND: MOVING BEYOND PERMISSION TO ENTITLEMENT

Katherine's hand trembled as she placed her luggage by the front door. "Are you sure you'll be okay?" she asked her husband Tom, who sat comfortably reading the newspaper. After twenty-six years of marriage and raising three children, this would be her first solo trip—a three-day writing workshop she'd dreamed about for years. She'd spent the previous week preparing meals, creating detailed schedules, and leaving emergency contact information, despite her youngest child having left for college eight months ago.

Tom lowered his newspaper. "Katherine, we've been through this. I managed a department of thirty people before retirement. I think I can manage myself for three days." He smiled, but Katherine still hesitated at the door.

"I know, but—"

"No buts," Tom said gently. "This isn't about permission anymore. This is your right. You've earned this."

Katherine nodded, though the concept still felt foreign. Permission she understood—the careful negotiation with guilt she'd practised over recent weeks. But entitlement? That word carried weight she wasn't sure she could bear.

What if you no longer needed to permit yourself at all? What if self-prioritisation became your baseline expectation rather than a conscious decision requiring justification? This shift—from needing permission to claiming entitlement—represents the final stage in your permission escalation journey and forms the foundation for your next chapter.

Many women hesitate at "entitlement," hearing echoes of selfishness or arrogance. Yet there's a world of difference between entitled self-prioritisation and self-centred behaviour. The entitlement you must embrace comes after decades of balancing others' needs with your own, often tipping the scales heavily toward others. It isn't about dismissing responsibilities or connections but recognising that after years of putting your children first, you've earned the right to prioritise yourself without guilt or apology.

I remember when Maria first came to our support group, having spent 22 years arranging her schedule around her children's activities, often postponing her interests. During our first session, she couldn't commit to a 15-minute walk without checking if anyone needed her. Six weeks into her permission journey, she finally booked a weekend painting retreat—something she'd wanted to do for years. Yet even after making the reservation, she created mental contingency plans: "If my daughter calls with an emergency, I'll leave right away," or "If my husband sounds too busy when I call to check in, I should probably come home early."

When I suggested that Maria might be entitled to a weekend entirely focused on herself, she looked shocked. "Entitled? That sounds so... selfish."

"Is it selfish," I asked her, "to claim something you've earned after two decades of putting others first?"

This question marks the threshold you now stand upon—the doorway between permission and entitlement. You must cross it to complete your transformation. In this chapter, I'll guide you through four essential steps that build upon each other to cement this mindset shift: first, crafting your personal Declaration of Entitlement; second, developing your legacy plan to balance wisdom-sharing with self-fulfilment; third, creating powerful visualisation practices that reinforce your entitled identity; and finally, preparing strategic responses to maintain your entitlement when facing inevitable resistance.

Crafting Your Declaration of Entitlement

When Katherine returned from her writing workshop, something had changed. She walked differently—shoulders back, chin lifted. She didn't immediately rush to clean or cook the first morning home. Instead, she poured herself a coffee and sat at the kitchen table with her journal.

"What are you writing?" Tom asked.

"My Declaration of Entitlement," she replied without looking up. "It's time."

A Declaration of Entitlement isn't wishful thinking—it's a formal acknowledgement of rights you've already earned through years of balanced caregiving.

Unlike permission statements that tentatively ask for optional concessions, entitlement statements boldly claim what is rightfully yours.

This shift in language might appear subtle, but it carries tremendous psychological power:

Permission Statement	Entitlement Statement
"I give myself permission to Prioritise my health needs this week."	"I am entitled to Prioritise my health needs as a non-negotiable life priority."
"I allow myself to decline additional family responsibilities when tired."	"I am entitled to maintain boundaries that protect my energy and well-being."
"I grant myself permission to explore a new interest even if it takes time away from family."	"I am entitled to pursue interests that fulfil me without justification or apology."

Do you see the difference? Permission statements typically include time limitations or specific conditions, while entitlement statements establish ongoing rights without qualification or expiration date. This linguistic transformation fundamentally reshapes your relationship with self-prioritisation.

You must now create your own Declaration of Entitlement. Here's precisely what you'll need:

- A dedicated notebook or special document on your computer
- 45-60 minutes of uninterrupted time (schedule this on your calendar now)
- The list of permission statements you've been working with throughout previous chapters

Step 1: Review and Identify Patterns

Begin by reviewing all the permission statements you've written during your journey. Look for recurring themes—areas you've consistently needed to permit yourself. These represent the domains where shifting to entitlement will have the most tremendous impact on your life.

Step 2: Draft Your Declaration

Now, draft your declaration using this proven framework:

1. **Opening statement** that acknowledges your years of caregiving while claiming your right to self-prioritisation

2. **Three to five specific entitlement statements** covering the area's most critical to your next chapter
3. **Supporting rationale** for each entitlement statement, connecting it to your identity as an architect of transitions
4. **Commitment statement** that expresses your intention to honour these entitlements from now on

I'll never forget when Diane, a 53-year-old former school volunteer coordinator in our support group, read her declaration aloud for the first time. Her voice shook at first, then strengthened with each word:

"After twenty-four years of nurturing my children's growth and development, I now claim my rightful entitlement to architect my next chapter with the same care and attention I've given to others. My identity as a mother continues, but no longer defines the boundaries of my choices or the allocation of my time, energy, and resources."

By the end, tears streamed down her face—not tears of sadness, but of recognition. The room fell silent, then erupted in applause.

Step 3: Revisit and Strengthen

Your Declaration of Entitlement isn't a one-and-done document. You must return to it weekly, reading it aloud (yes, actually speaking the words) and making adjustments as your comfort with entitlement grows. Most women discover their declarations become stronger and more expansive with each revision as they shed lingering guilt and fully embrace their authentic identity.

Developing Your Legacy Plan

"But if I'm not constantly available to my kids, how will I pass down everything they still need to know?" During our next session, Maria asked, clutching her newly written Declaration of Entitlement. Her question revealed one of the most common barriers to embracing entitlement: the fear that stepping back means abandoning your responsibility to transmit wisdom, values, and life lessons to your children.

This concern creates a false choice: either remain in your primary caregiving role or surrender your legacy influence entirely. The truth lies elsewhere.

Maria invited her adult children to Sunday dinner three months after writing her Declaration. After dessert, she brought out a worn recipe box.

"These are your grandmother's recipes," she explained, "and some are from her mother. I want to teach you how to make these dishes—one recipe each month when you visit." She paused. "Not because I have to, but because I want to share this part of our family history with you."

Her son looked surprised. "I'd like that, Mom. But I thought you were trying to do less family stuff now."

Maria smiled. "I'm entitled to share what matters to me and have my own life. That's what my legacy plan is about."

A personal legacy plan resolves the conflict between self-prioritisation and wisdom transmission by creating structured approaches that honour both needs simultaneously. Your legacy doesn't require constant availability—it thrives with intentional, bounded sharing.

Now you must create your legacy plan by answering four critical questions:

1. What specific wisdom, values, or life lessons do you most want to transmit?
2. Which transmission methods will be most effective with your particular adult children?
3. How can you share your legacy while respecting boundaries and independent decision-making?
4. What schedule or structure allows meaningful sharing without dominating your next chapter?

After answering these questions, consider these proven legacy transmission methods and how they align with your entitled next chapter:

- **Scheduled wisdom conversations** — Monthly dinners or coffee meetings specifically dedicated to sharing experiences and insights when adult children are receptive
- **Written legacy documents** — Letters, journals, or guided memoirs that capture your most important life lessons without requiring immediate response
- **Skill transmission workshops** — Teaching sessions where you share specific expertise (cooking family recipes, financial management, home maintenance) in a structured, time-limited way

- **Family history projects** — Collaborative efforts to document family stories and heritage that create a legacy without daily involvement
- **Values-aligned experiences** — Shared activities that demonstrate values in action rather than through direct instruction

I'll never forget Rebecca's brilliant solution when she faced this challenge. She worried that geographic distance would prevent meaningful legacy transmission, as she had two adult daughters living several states away. During our work together, she developed her quarterly "wisdom package"—a small box she mailed to each daughter containing a letter about a specific life lesson, a relevant book or token, and an invitation to discuss by phone when convenient.

"The first time I sent them, I was nervous," Rebecca told our group. "I worried they'd see it as intrusive or weird." She laughed. "But my younger daughter called immediately and said it was the most meaningful gift she'd ever received. Now they both look forward to them."

This structured approach allowed Rebecca to share essential insights while respecting her daughters' independence and honouring her entitled time.

Your legacy plan must include specific timeframes, methods, and topics, creating clear boundaries that fulfil this important function without sacrificing your entitled self-prioritisation. The most effective legacy transmission follows a simple rule: quality over quantity. A thoughtful, well-timed piece of wisdom typically has more impact than years of constant availability or unsolicited advice.

Creating Visualisation Practices for Your Entitled Future Self

Katherine sat in her favourite chair, eyes closed, breathing deeply. After writing her Declaration of Entitlement, she'd committed to daily visualisation practice and today marked day fifteen.

"How's it going?" I asked when she arrived for our session later that week.

"Strange," she admitted. "My mind knows I'm entitled to make choices, but my emotions haven't caught up. The first few times I visualised saying no to my daughter's last-minute requests, my heart raced, and I felt sick to my stomach—even though it was just in my imagination!"

"And now?" I prompted.

A slow smile spread across her face. Yesterday, I visualised booking a solo vacation. It is a weekend workshop and a two-week painting retreat in Italy. In my visualisation, I felt... peaceful. Excited. Not guilty."

"That's how it works," I explained. "Your intellectual mind grasps entitlement quickly, but your emotional mind, conditioned by decades of putting others first, needs more convincing. These visualisation practices are rewiring your brain."

You must now establish your visualisation practice to bridge this gap between intellectual understanding and emotional acceptance. Effective visualisation combines detailed mental imagery with emotional engagement, creating neural pathways that support your entitled identity at both conscious and subconscious levels.

Begin with this basic daily practice:

1. Find a quiet space where you won't be interrupted for 10-15 minutes.
2. Close your eyes and take several deep breaths to centre yourself.
3. Imagine yourself one year from now, fully embodying your entitled identity.
4. Notice specific details: How do you carry yourself? How do you respond when someone demands your time? What daily rituals reflect your entitlement?
5. Most importantly, how does it feel to live from this entitled place? Allow yourself to fully experience this future self's confidence, freedom, and purposefulness.

Jennifer's story perfectly illustrates the power of this practice. At 56, this empty nester had struggled with boundary-setting her entire life. During her visualisation practice, she created a detailed mental scene of her future self-confidently saying, "That won't work for me", when her adult son asked her to rearrange her schedule to babysit with no advance notice.

"The first time I visualised this scene," Jennifer told our group, "My hands were shaking, and I felt this knot in my stomach—just from imagining saying no!" She laughed. "But I kept Practising the same scene every day for a week. By day seven, I visualised myself saying no calmly, and instead of anxiety, I felt ...proud. Strong."

Jennifer's son called three days later with a last-minute babysitting request that conflicted with her watercolour class. She hesitantly replied, "I'm sorry, that won't work for me. I commit." She described the experience as "surreal—like my visualisation had prepared me so thoroughly that my body knew what to do before my mind could start arguing."

For maximum impact, you must practice visualisation daily, following this progression:

Days 1-7: Focus on simple boundary-setting scenarios **Days 8-14:** Expand to visualising how you Prioritise your needs in multiple relationships **Days 15-21:** Advance to imagining allocating significant resources (time, money, energy) to personal interests **Days 22-28:** Culminate with visualising yourself making major life decisions based primarily on your desires rather than others' expectations

Document each visualisation experience in your Permission Journal, noting how your emotional response changes. You'll likely discover that scenarios initially triggering intense guilt gradually become normalised through consistent practice. This emotional shift is evidence of your brain creating new neural pathways that support your entitled identity.

Maintaining Entitlement When Facing Resistance

Maria's phone rang at 10:30 PM on the second night of her painting retreat. Her daughter's name flashed on the screen. Her hand hovered over the phone, heart racing. She would have answered immediately in the past months, already mentally packing her bags to rush home. Tonight was different.

She took a deep breath, remembered her visualisation practice, and answered calmly.

"Mom, I bombed my interview today," her daughter said, voice cracking. "I need to talk it through. Can you come home early tomorrow instead of Sunday?"

Old guilt surged through Maria's body. But instead of immediately agreeing, she paused.

"I hear you're disappointed about the interview," Maria said with genuine empathy. "That's tough. I'm confident you'll figure out the next steps, and I look forward to hearing what you decide when I return Sunday evening as planned."

The call ended with her daughter frustrated but intact, and Maria still firmly at her retreat.

Later that week in our group session, Maria shared, "When I hung up, I felt this wave of guilt. But I repeated my mantra: 'My entitlement is earned, not taken.' By morning, the guilt had passed, and I enjoyed my final day fully present. The amazing thing? When I got home, my daughter had already figured out a solution and was fine."

As you shift from permission-seeking to entitled self-direction, you will encounter resistance. This isn't a possibility—it's a certainty. Resistance will come from three sources: family members accustomed to your constant availability, friends who don't understand your transformation, and most powerfully, from your internalised guilt voice.

You must prepare for this resistance now, before it happens, to maintain your entitlement stance when challenged. The most effective preparation strategy combines awareness, language preparation, and response rehearsal.

Step 1: Cultivate Awareness

First, acknowledge that resistance is typical and expected. When you change patterns established over decades, others naturally react with confusion or pushback. This doesn't signal you're doing something wrong—quite the opposite. Resistance often indicates your transformation is meaningful enough to disrupt established dynamics. Expect, recognise, and view it as confirmation that you're making significant changes.

Step 2: Prepare Your Language

Next, you must prepare specific language for different types of resistance. When caught off guard, most women revert to people-pleasing responses. Having pre-crafted statements prevents this backsliding:

Step 3: Practice Response Rehearsal

Finally, you must rehearse these responses mentally through visualisation and verbally through role-play with a supportive friend. Rehearsal builds neural pathways that make confident responses accessible when you're under pressure, when your emotional brain might otherwise override your rational intentions.

Knowing her daughter might call during her retreat, Maria had role-played responses to various scenarios with me during our session. This preparation allowed her to respond empathetically while maintaining her boundary when the call came.

The most persistent resistance often comes from your own internalised guilt voice. Katherine described this as "the voice that's been with me so long, it sounds more like me than my thoughts." You must address this by creating a specific "entitlement mantra"—a brief statement that directly counters your particular flavour of guilt.

Choose one of these proven mantras or create your own:
- "My self-care enables better care for others."
- "My entitlement is earned, not taken."
- "My needs matter equally to others' wants."
- "My next chapter requires self-prioritisation."

Repeat your chosen mantra whenever guilt arises, reinforcing your entitled mindset until it becomes your default perspective rather than a conscious choice.

As you complete this final stage of your permission escalation journey, recognise the significant transformation you've achieved. From tentative 15-minute permission exercises to confident entitlement statements, you've systematically dismantled decades of self-sacrifice conditioning and established yourself as the architect of your next chapter.

This shift from permission to entitlement creates the psychological foundation for everything that follows—from purposeful time structures to redesigned relationships to meaningful contribution. With entitlement as your baseline, you're now positioned to explore the practical domains of your empty nest transformation with confidence and clarity.

Katherine called to share her news six months after completing her entitlement work. "I've registered for a year-long art certification program," she said, excitement bubbling in her voice. "It meets every Tuesday and Thursday, and I didn't ask anyone's permission or check anyone's schedule before signing up." She paused. "I just did it because I wanted to. Because I'm entitled to."

This is the freedom that awaits you beyond the entitlement threshold.

In the next chapter, we'll build on this entitlement foundation to architect your purpose portfolio—creating multiple sources of meaning and motivation that generate the same sense of significance your parenting role once provided. With your entitlement firmly established, you're ready to design daily structures that generate authentic fulfilment in this new chapter of your life.

Chapter 11

ARCHITECTING YOUR PURPOSE PORTFOLIO

Sarah woke at 3 AM, the house silent in a way that felt wrong after six months.

She padded the hallway past her son's empty bedroom, trailing her fingers along the wall where height marks still charted his growth. The kitchen calendar mocked her with its abundance of neatly written appointments—yoga, book club, volunteer shifts, lunch dates—yet beneath this carefully constructed busyness lurked a void no activity seemed to fill. Last week, sitting in her car after another enjoyable but somehow hollow book club meeting, she'd finally whispered the truth she'd been avoiding: "I don't know who I am without them needing me."

This moment—this precise confrontation with the difference between filling time and finding purpose—marks the threshold you now stand upon as an empty nester. You've claimed permission through the GRANT framework. You've moved from tentative self-authorisation to genuine entitlement. Now comes the most crucial application of that entitlement: architecting a life of purpose that generates the same profound sense of meaning your parenting role once provided.

How Purpose Differs from Merely Staying Busy

Ellen stood frozen in her kitchen at 7:30 PM on a Tuesday, staring at the wall calendar she'd proudly filled with activities after her twins left for college.

"I don't understand," she told me during our coaching session, her voice cracking. "I'm doing everything the articles said. I joined groups. I volunteered. I reconnected with friends. My schedule is fuller than when the kids lived at home. Why do I still feel like something huge is missing?"

The tremor in Ellen's voice will sound familiar if you've attempted to replace your parenting role with random activities. You must understand this crucial distinction: busyness and purpose exist in different dimensions. Busyness occupies time; purpose creates meaning. Busyness fills your calendar; purpose fills your soul.

This isn't just philosophical wordplay—it's the difference between a hollow retirement and a genuinely fulfilling next chapter.

True purpose contains four elements chronically absent from mere busyness:

1. **Significance**: Activities that matter beyond simple completion
2. **Growth**: Opportunities that stretch your capabilities
3. **Contribution**: Ways to impact others or your community
4. **Enjoyment**: Genuine pleasure in the experience itself

A pattern emerged when Ellen examined her packed calendar through this four-element lens. Her volunteer work teaching adults to read contained all four elements—it mattered deeply, challenged her to develop new teaching skills, clearly helped others, and brought her genuine joy. But her book club, yoga class, and lunch dates merely filled hours without creating meaning.

You've experienced the power of purpose through your parenting years. Every diaper changed, every homework assignment supervised, every teenage crisis navigated contained all four elements of purpose. Your daily tasks mattered profoundly. You constantly grew through new challenges. Your contribution to your children's development was unmistakable. And despite the difficulties, you found deep joy in witnessing their growth.

No random activity can match that. And it shouldn't have to.

You must now permit yourself to architect something different but equally meaningful—your purpose portfolio.

The Journey to Multiple-Purpose Areas

The most damaging myth you face as an empty nester is that you must find a single replacement purpose that is as meaningful as parenting. This creates impossible pressure and inevitable disappointment. Stop this search immediately. No single activity can replicate the multidimensional purpose that parenting provides.

Maria's story illustrates the trap—and the way out.

A former stay-at-home mother of three boys, Maria spent six months after her youngest left for college in a frantic search for her "next purpose." She volunteered at the hospital, took painting classes, and even considered returning to school. Nothing felt significant enough.

"I want something as meaningful as raising my children was," she explained during our first session, frustration evident in her voice. "But everything I try feels trivial by comparison."

Through our work together, Maria realised she was asking the wrong question. Rather than "What single activity can replace parenting?" she needed to ask, "What combination of pursuits can create a meaningful life?"

This shift in perspective changed everything.

Your purpose portfolio must include elements from multiple domains:

- **Creative Expression**: Activities that allow you to make or build something uniquely yours
- **Knowledge Pursuit**: Learning opportunities that expand your understanding
- **Physical Challenges**: Endeavours that engage your body and physical capabilities
- **Relationship Cultivation**: Connections that create mutual growth
- **Spiritual Development**: Practices that nurture your inner life
- **Community Contribution**: Service that improves others' lives
- **Professional Engagement**: Work that utilises your skills and experience

The strength of this portfolio approach lies in its diversity. When one purpose area temporarily fails to inspire (as all purposes occasionally do), others sustain you. This creates emotional resilience unavailable to those seeking a single perfect replacement for parenting.

For Maria, the breakthrough came when she stopped trying to find the "next big thing" and instead built a portfolio across several domains. Her weekly schedule evolved to include:

- **Mondays and Wednesdays**: Teaching ESL classes to recent immigrants (community contribution)
- **Tuesdays**: Advanced Spanish courses at the community college (knowledge pursuit)
- **Thursdays**: Hiking with a women's group (physical challenge)
- **Friday mornings**: Mentoring new mothers through her church (relationship cultivation)

"No single activity matches what parenting gave me," she told me six months later, her eyes bright with renewed purpose. "But together, they create a life that feels rich and meaningful in a completely different way."

This is your path forward as well. You don't need one perfect purpose—you need a balanced portfolio of meaningful engagements.

Using the Meaning Matrix to Evaluate Options

Having permitted yourself to explore multiple purpose areas, you now face a new challenge: with unlimited possibilities, how do you choose which activities deserve inclusion in your purpose portfolio?

James's story illuminates this critical phase of your journey.

When James's youngest daughter left for college—coinciding with his early retirement from executive leadership—he faced what he called "a double identity crisis." Without his career or active parenting role, he felt completely adrift.

"I could do anything," he said during our first coaching session. "That's the problem. With so many options, I'm paralysed by indecision."

You likely feel this same paralysis. The Meaning Matrix will guide you through it, as it helped James.

The Meaning Matrix evaluates potential purpose areas across four dimensions that predict genuine fulfilment rather than temporary distraction:

Dimension	Question to Ask	Low Score (1-3)	High Score (8-10)
Personal Significance	How meaningful is this to me personally?	"Seems like something I should do"	"This matters deeply to me"
Skill Utilization	Does this use capabilities I value in myself?	"Anyone could do this"	"This uses my unique strengths"

Growth Potential	Will this help me develop new aspects of myself?	"I already know how to do this"	"This will stretch me in new ways"
Contribution Impact	Does this positively affect others or the world?	"This only benefits me"	"This creates value beyond myself"

To use the Meaning Matrix in your purpose exploration:

1. Make a list of activities that interest you.
2. Assign a score from 1-10 in each activity in each dimension.
3. Add the four scores to get a total Meaning Score for each activity.
4. Consider activities scoring 30+ for your purpose portfolio.
5. Eliminate or reconsider activities scoring under 20.

This systematic evaluation prevented James from making a common empty-nester mistake. His initial plan—joining a golf league to fill time—scored only 17 on the Meaning Matrix. It would occupy hours but leave him feeling hollow.

Instead, three activities emerged with scores above 30:

- Mentoring young entrepreneurs through the SBA (33)
- Taking woodworking classes to build furniture for a homeless shelter (35)
- Teaching business courses at the community college (31)

James started with the woodworking classes, then gradually added the other high-scoring activities over six months. One year later, he reported feeling more purposeful than at any point in his career.

"The Matrix forced me to be honest about what would create genuine meaning, not just fill calendar slots," he explained.

The process will do the same for you. Trust the scores, even when they contradict what you "should" want. The activities scoring highest on your personal Meaning Matrix form the foundation of your unique purpose portfolio.

Building a Balanced Purpose Portfolio

As your purpose portfolio takes shape, you must ensure balance across different purposes. This final step creates sustainability through inevitable life changes.

Claire's story reveals the danger of an unbalanced portfolio—and the path to greater resilience.

After her empty nest, Claire built what seemed like a perfect purpose portfolio centred entirely around her church community. She led women's groups, organised meal trains, taught Sunday school, and coordinated outreach programs. Each activity scored high on the Meaning Matrix, and for the first year, she felt deeply fulfilled.

Then her husband's job transferred them to another state.

"I lost everything at once," Claire told me after reaching out for emergency coaching. "Not just my community, but every single purpose I'd built. I had to start completely over."

Her experience highlights why your purpose portfolio must balance:

1. **Portable purposes** that travel with you regardless of location.
2. **Rooted purposes** tied to specific communities or settings.

It must also balance:

1. **Social purposes** that involve connection with others.
2. **Solo purposes** you can pursue independently.

This dual-axis balance creates resilience against inevitable changes that might otherwise devastate your sense of meaning.

After her difficult transition, Claire rebuilt her portfolio with greater balance across all quadrants:

	Social	Solo
Portable	Online grief support group moderator	Writing children's stories
Rooted	New church community service	Local botanical garden volunteering

"Now if something changes—if we move again or if my health changes—I won't lose everything at once," she explained. "I've built a purpose that can adapt with me."

Your purpose portfolio should contain a minimum of four different purpose areas, with at least one in each quadrant of this portable/rooted and social/solo matrix. This ensures that no single life change can simultaneously eliminate all your sources of meaning.

For James, the executive-turned-woodworker we met earlier, this meant consciously balancing his portfolio:

	Social	Solo
Portable	Online business consulting	Woodworking projects
Rooted	Community college teaching	Local hiking challenges

Follow this same strategic approach to build your balanced purpose portfolio:

1. **Week 1**: Identify 10+ potential purpose areas that interest you.
2. **Week 2**: Evaluate each using the Meaning Matrix.
3. **Week 3**: Select your highest-scoring options, ensuring at least one in each quadrant.
4. **Week 4**: Begin with one purpose area that excites you most.
5. **Months 2-6**: Gradually add the others until your portfolio is complete.

Your purpose portfolio doesn't need to be built overnight. Start with one purpose area that scores highest on your Meaning Matrix, then gradually add others over six months. The goal is sustainable fulfilment, not immediate replacement for your lost parenting purpose.

Remember: Your identity was never just a parent but always an architect of meaningful transitions. The same capabilities that made you an excellent parent—vision, dedication, nurturing, problem-solving—now equip you to design a purpose portfolio as meaningful as your parenting years, but centred on your entitled self-direction rather than others' needs.

In the coming weeks, the purpose portfolio you design will transform empty nest freedom from theoretical to tangible. It will replace the hollow busyness that leaves you empty with genuine meaning that fills your soul. Most importantly, it will create the daily motivation and significance you've missed since your children left home.

In the next chapter, we'll build on this foundation by exploring how to redesign relationships with adult children, spouse, and friends to support your new purpose-driven identity while maintaining meaningful connections. After all, the architect of transitions doesn't just design purpose—they also redesign relationships.

Chapter 12

RELATIONSHIP REDESIGN

Sarah stood frozen in her kitchen, phone in hand, thumb hovering over the call button. Three days had passed since her son Jake mentioned his roommate conflict, and she'd drafted—then deleted—seven text messages offering advice.

"What do I say that doesn't sound like I'm treating him like a child?" she whispered. Before the empty nest, she would have told him what to do. Now, everything felt different. This moment of hesitation marked the crossroads between two identities—the authority figure she'd been for twenty years and the trusted advisor she hoped to become.

This chapter guides you through deliberately redesigning your most essential relationships, transforming them from anchors to your past identity into bridges to your future self. The relationships you cultivate now will either support your emergence as an architect of transitions or keep you tethered to outdated patterns that no longer serve you.

Transforming Parent-Child Relationships into Adult Connections
Elena arrived at my workshop with dark circles under her eyes. "I haven't slept properly since Megan left for college," she confessed to the group. "Not because I miss her, though I do, but because I don't know who I am to her anymore. Yesterday, she called about a professor she's struggling with, and I jumped into problem-solving mode. She cut me off and said, 'Mom, I'm just venting. I don't need you to fix it.' I felt completely useless."

The room filled with knowing nods. This painful moment of recognition—that your children need something different from you now—marks the beginning of relationship transformation rather than its end.

The most significant barrier to building adult relationships with your children isn't physical distance but psychological transition. You must shift from an authority figure to a trusted advisor, from a director to a consultant, and from a manager to a mentor. This evolution doesn't happen automatically when your child moves out—it requires deliberate redesign.

Begin with an honest assessment of your current communication patterns:

Communication Pattern	What It Sounds Like	Adult Relationship Impact
Authority-Based	"You should join the marketing club to get a good job."	Creates resistance and distance
Information-Monitoring	"Did you go to class today? What about your laundry? Are you eating enough?"	Signals distrust of their capabilities
Emotional Caretaking	"Don't worry about that professor. I'll email the department head."	Undermines their independence
Reciprocal Exchange	"That situation sounds frustrating. When I faced something similar, I tried... What do you think might work?"	Builds mutual respect
Interest-Driven	"I saw a documentary on that topic you're studying. What's your take on it?"	Develops a multidimensional relationship

Michael, a father of two college students, shared his breakthrough during our third coaching session: "I realised I've been stuck in authority mode for so long, I didn't know another way to communicate. Before I call my son, I say aloud, 'I give myself permission to be interested without directing.' Our conversations have completely changed."

The permission framework offers powerful tools for navigating this territory with confidence:

Permission Statements for Parent-Child Evolution

When you notice yourself slipping into outdated patterns, pause and silently recite these bridge statements:

1. "I give myself permission to let you handle this situation your way."
2. "I give myself permission to share my experience without expecting you to follow my advice."

3. "I give myself permission to trust your judgment even when it differs from mine."
4. "I give myself permission to enjoy our relationship as it evolves rather than clinging to how it was."

These statements create psychological space between your instinctive reaction and communication, allowing you to choose responses that support adult connection rather than reinforce dependency.

Karen, a workshop participant, described her transformation: "My daughter called about a work conflict, and I felt that familiar urge to solve everything. Instead, I silently told myself, 'I give myself permission to listen without fixing.' What happened next amazed me—she seemed to open up more, and by the end of the call, she'd worked through her solution. I realised she mostly needed a sounding board, not a problem-solver."

Next, identify the boundaries that healthy adult relationships require:

Boundary Recognition Exercise

Complete this three-column exercise to identify needed boundaries in your parent-child relationship:

Area	My Current Behaviour	Appropriate Adult Boundary
Financial assistance	Automatically cover unexpected expenses	Discuss the need and options before offering help
Uninvited advice	Share opinions on decisions, large and small	Wait to be asked before offering a perspective
Contact frequency	Expect daily communication	Allow natural communication rhythms to develop
Information sharing	Ask detailed questions about all aspects	Share about myself and follow their lead on details
Home visits	Expect holiday attendance regardless of circumstances	Negotiate visit timing with respect for their commitments

The transition to adult relationships doesn't mean abandoning parental wisdom or care—it means expressing these qualities within appropriate boundaries that honour your children's independence.

Rebuilding Intimacy and Partnership with Your Spouse

The dining room felt cavernous with just the two sitting at opposite ends of the table. Teresa pushed her food around her plate while Michael scrolled through his phone.

"So," Teresa ventured after several minutes of silence.

"So," Michael replied, not looking up.

"Is this what it's going to be like now?" she asked quietly.

Michael finally put down his phone and met her eyes. "I don't know what to talk about when it's not about the kids."

This moment, painful as it was, marked the beginning of something potentially extraordinary—the opportunity to rediscover each other beyond their parenting roles.

The empty nest often reveals the actual state of your marriage, stripped of the logistical partnership that raising children required. Many couples face an uncomfortable discovery: they've been excellent co-parents but forgotten how to be partners.

Begin by taking stock of your current relationship dynamics:

Dimension	Co-Parent Status	Partnership Status
Conversation topics	"Did you sign the permission slip?" "Who's picking up from soccer?"	"What did you think about that article?" "Tell me about your day."
Time allocation	Coordinating children's schedules, attending their events	Planned a couple of activities, shared experiences
Decision-making	"Which summer camp works best?" "How should we handle this teacher issue?"	"What are our goals for the next five years?" "How do we want to grow together?"
Intimacy	Scheduled around children's activities, often deprioritised	Regular connection through physical and emotional intimacy
Future planning	College funds, children's milestone events	Couple dreams, shared adventures, and supporting individual growth

Jennifer and David sat uncomfortably across from each other at a restaurant table on their first "empty nest date." Jennifer nervously twisted her napkin. "This feels like a first date, except we've been married 26 years."

David nodded. "I know. I keep trying to think of something to say that isn't about the kids."

After a long pause, Jennifer took a deep breath and said, "Maybe that's okay. Maybe we need to get to know each other again."

That simple acknowledgement became the first step in their marriage renaissance.

The permission framework can transform your partnership when applied jointly:

1. "We give ourselves permission to rediscover each other beyond our parenting roles."
2. "We give ourselves permission to Prioritise our relationship without feeling guilty."
3. "We give ourselves permission to create new traditions and experiences together."
4. "We give ourselves permission to evolve our relationship in ways that support our needs."

Jennifer and David created a weekly "permission date" where they experimented with new activities and conversation topics that were explicitly unrelated to their children. "It felt awkward at first," Jennifer shared six months later, "but we discovered things we'd forgotten or never known about each other. I'm more interested in him now than I've been in years."

To rebuild your connection, start with this Interest Excavation Exercise:

1. Individually list interests you had before children.
2. Identify current interests that excite you.
3. Share your lists and circle overlapping items.
4. Select one overlapping interest to explore together this week.

The goal isn't to erase your identities as parents but to add dimensions to your relationship that aren't dependent on that role.

Creating Friendship Circles Beyond Parenting Networks

Patricia sat alone on Saturday morning, scrolling through social media. Her feed showed groups of women hiking, having brunch, attending concerts—all things she'd love to do. She closed the app with a sigh.

"Who would I even go with?" she wondered aloud. Her coffee group had disbanded when their children graduated from high school, and she realised all her friends were just the mothers of her daughter's friends. When they stopped seeing each other at school events, the connections faded.

"How do I make friends just like me?" she whispered. "Not as Alexis's mom, but as Patricia?"

The social isolation many empty nesters experience stems from a simple reality: most friendships were built around their children's activities and school connections. As those structures disappear, so do the natural opportunities for social interaction.

Adult friendships typically form around shared elements:

Friendship Domain	Examples	Permission Action
Activity-Based	Fitness classes, sports leagues, and walking groups	"I give myself permission to join a group activity even if I go alone."
Interest-Based	Book clubs, cooking classes, and gardening groups	"I give myself permission to pursue interests I previously set aside."
Value-Based	Volunteer organisations, religious communities, and advocacy groups	"I give myself permission to dedicate time to causes I care about."
Proximity-Based	Neighbours, local community centres, and nearby venues	"I give myself permission to initiate contact with people I see regularly."

Elizabeth stood outside the community centre, gripping her yoga mat so tightly her knuckles turned white. "This is ridiculous," she muttered to herself. "I'm 54 and terrified to walk into a beginner's yoga class." She closed her eyes and repeated, "I permit myself to feel awkward. I permit myself to feel awkward."

She didn't expect the permission statement to eliminate her anxiety, and it didn't. But it made the anxiety acceptable instead of shameful. She took a deep breath and pulled open the door.

Two months later, Elizabeth had a regular walking partner from that class and had been to coffee with three other women. "The awkwardness didn't go away," she reported, "but my permission to feel it made it bearable enough to keep showing up."

Counter friendship-building hesitation with specific permission statements:

1. "I give myself permission to prioritise building friendships that support my current identity."
2. "I allow myself to feel awkward during the friendship-building process."
3. "I give myself permission to invite someone to coffee even if they might decline."

4. "I give myself permission to invest time in relationships that energise and support me."

Building new friendship circles requires deliberate effort and—you guessed it—permission to prioritise your social needs even when it feels uncomfortable.

Communicating Your Evolving Identity to Family and Friends

Robert sat at his sister's kitchen table, his stomach in knots. "I'm not hosting Thanksgiving this year," he finally said. "Linda and I are going to Santa Fe instead."

His sister stared at him. "But you've always done Thanksgiving! The whole family counts on it. The kids will be so disappointed."

Robert took a deep breath. "Susan, my 'kids' are 25 and 28—and they've made other plans this year."

"Well, what about Mom? And the cousins? Everyone expects Thanksgiving at your house."

This moment captures many empty nesters' challenge in communicating identity changes to those who benefit from your established patterns. Your permission framework gives you powerful tools to communicate your evolving identity in ways that invite understanding rather than resistance.

Use this progressive approach to help others adjust to your changing identity:

Stage	Communication Approach	Example
Awareness	Signal that changes are coming without requesting immediate acceptance	"Now that the kids are on their own, I'm exploring new directions for myself."
Education	Help others understand your internal journey.	"This transition has me thinking about who I am beyond being a parent and what I want my next chapter to look like."
Boundary Setting	Communicate new parameters	"I can no longer babysit every weekend as I've joined a Saturday hiking group that is important to me."
Invitation	Offer ways for them to connect with your evolving self	"I'd love to share this new interest with you if you want to join me sometime."

Lynn stood in her empty living room, surrounded by boxes. Her son Adam leaned against the doorframe, arms crossed.

"I still don't understand why you need to sell the house," he said. "It's been our home for twenty years."

Lynn felt the familiar tug of guilt but remembered her permission statement: "I give myself permission to make decisions that support my next chapter."

"I know this is hard," she said gently. "This house holds wonderful memories for all of us. And I'm ready for a place that fits who I am now, not who I was when raising three children. The condo downtown gives me walking access to everything I love, and the maintenance-free living means I can travel more."

Adam's expression softened slightly. "I just never pictured you anywhere but here."

"I know," Lynn nodded. "It's an adjustment for all of us. And I'm excited about this next chapter. I hope you'll visit the new place once I'm settled—there's a great coffee shop around the corner, I think you'd love."

Six months later, Adam admitted the smaller place suited her better, and they'd established a new tradition of meeting at that coffee shop when he visited.

When facing resistance to your changes, rely on these permission statements:

1. "I give myself permission to evolve even if others are uncomfortable with my changes."
2. "I allow myself to set boundaries that support my growth."
3. "I give myself permission to be misunderstood temporarily as I navigate this transition."
4. "I give myself permission to communicate my needs clearly without excessive justification."

These statements help you remain steadfast in your transformation even when facing pushback from those accustomed to your previous patterns.

**

As the sun set over her new neighbourhood, Sarah finally pressed the call button on her phone. When Jake answered, she immediately resisted asking about the roommate situation.

"I've been thinking about what you mentioned the other day," she said carefully. "That sounds like a challenging situation. Would it help to talk through it, or were you letting me know what's happening?"

The slight pause before Jake responded felt significant. "If you have time, I could use another perspective."

Sarah smiled, recognising this moment for what it was—the first steps on a bridge between their past relationship and the adult connection they were building. "I've got all the time in the world," she said, settling into her chair. "Tell me what you're thinking."

As you redesign your relationships during this transition, remember that the most important relationship change occurs within yourself, moving from seeing yourself as a supporting character to recognising yourself as the author of your story. This internal shift naturally extends to how you relate to others, creating space for connections that honour who you've been and are becoming.

Your relationship redesign isn't about abandoning meaningful connections but ensuring they evolve alongside you. Applying your permission framework to these important relationships creates the foundation for connections that will support and enhance your next chapter.

Chapter 13

TIME ARCHITECTURE MASTERY

Rachel's alarm clock buzzed at 6:15 a.m., just as it had for the past eighteen years.

She reached to silence it, then froze mid-motion as reality washed over her: there were no lunches to pack, no permission slips to sign, no sleepy teenagers to drag from bed. Her youngest had left for college three weeks ago, leaving her mornings structureless for the first time in nearly two decades. The silence of the house pressed against her ears like a physical weight.

"What's the point of getting up?" she whispered to the empty room.

Rachel's experience mirrors what countless empty nesters discover: the paradox of time wealth. After years of fantasising about having more personal time during the chaotic parenting years, the sudden abundance creates more anxiety than their previously overscheduled lives ever did. Where children's needs once provided natural structure and purpose, many new empty nesters now face formless days that somehow feel endlessly vacant and oddly rushed.

Creating Flexible Weekly Schedule Templates

"I should be thrilled with all this freedom," Sarah confessed during our group coaching session, clutching her pristine calendar. "Instead, I feel like I'm drowning in empty hours."

Around the room, heads nodded in understanding. After twenty-three years of scheduling her life around her children's needs, Sarah now faced weeks without a single obligation related to them—no soccer practices, no science fair projects, no parent-teacher conferences. The blank calendar that should have represented freedom instead triggered a profound disorientation.

"Last Tuesday, I sat in my car in the garage for twenty minutes, unable to decide what to do next," she admitted, her voice cracking slightly. "I had the whole day ahead of me and absolutely no idea how to fill it."

The group's reaction was immediate—knowing glances, sympathetic murmurs, the relief of shared experience. Sarah wasn't describing weakness or confusion; she was articulating a universal empty nest challenge that few discuss openly: without children's external structure, many parents struggle to architect their newfound time.

This struggle stems from a common misconception: that freedom from schedules means freedom from structure. Effective time architecture requires thoughtful frameworks that guide without restricting, providing direction while preserving the spontaneity that makes this life stage unique.

Your journey to time mastery begins with creating weekly schedule templates that serve as flexible blueprints rather than rigid commands. Unlike the non-negotiable commitments of your parenting years, these templates function as guiding structures that can evolve as your needs and interests change.

The Four Pillars of Weekly Architecture

Your weekly template should balance four essential elements:

1. **Anchor activities** – Regular commitments that provide dependable structure

Examples: Weekly fitness classes, volunteer shifts, and standing social engagements

"My Thursday morning pottery class became my first anchor point," explained Michael, a former coaching client whose two children left for college in the same year. "Knowing I had somewhere specific to be at 9 a.m. gave that day a sense of purpose the others lacked."

2. **Focus blocks** – Protected time for priority projects aligned with your purpose portfolio

Examples: Writing sessions, business development, creative projects

"I blocked Mondays and Wednesdays from 1-4 p.m. for my photography," shared Elena, whose empty nest coincided with her decision to pursue a long-postponed passion. "Having those hours specifically designated makes me treat this work as legitimate rather than just a hobby I'll get to 'someday.'"

3. **Connection periods** – Dedicated times for nurturing key relationships

Examples: Date nights, friend meetups, scheduled calls with adult children

"We schedule our marriage now," laughed Robert, five months into his empty nest journey. "Every Friday night is protected for us, no exceptions. It feels strange to schedule time with my wife after 27 years together formally, but it's been transformative."

4. **White space** – Unscheduled time that allows for spontaneity and recovery

Examples: Mornings without appointments, afternoons left intentionally open

"Learning to leave blank space in my calendar was the hardest part," admitted Jennifer, eighteen months into her empty nest. "I kept feeling compelled to fill every hour. Now I protect my Tuesday and Thursday afternoons as sacred white space—time that belongs to me with no predetermined purpose."

When building your weekly template, avoid the common mistake of filling every available hour—a habit many empty nesters carry forward from their overscheduled parenting years. Instead, recognise that proper time architecture requires structure and space, much like a well-designed home needs walls and open areas to feel balanced.

Time Element	Purpose	Why It Matters	Permission Statement
Anchor Activities	Provide a reliable structure	Creates momentum and reduces decision fatigue	"I give myself permission to create dependable structure through consistent commitments."
Focus Blocks	Advance priority projects	Ensures progress on meaningful work	"I authorise myself to protect uninterrupted time for my most important pursuits."
Connection Periods	Nurture key relationships	Prevents relationships from falling to the bottom of the list	"I am entitled to schedule quality time with the people who matter most."
White Space	Allow for spontaneity and recovery	Creates breathing room for emerging interests and rest	"I deserve blank space in my calendar with no predetermined purpose."

Building Your First Template

Begin with a blank weekly grid and follow this sequence:

1. First, position your non-negotiable anchor activities

2. Next, schedule 2-3 focus blocks for priority projects
3. Then, allocate specific times for key relationships
4. Finally, preserve at least 30% of your available time as white space

"The first template I created lasted exactly eight days before I completely abandoned it," laughed Carol, now six months into her empty nest journey. "I'd overstructured everything based on what I thought I should be doing rather than what energised me. The second version was much simpler and far more sustainable."

Carol's experience highlights a crucial point: your initial template is a starting point, not a permanent solution. Expect to revise it several times as you discover which structures truly support your empty nest freedom.

Establishing Daily Rituals That Provide Structure and Meaning

The morning after her youngest daughter left for college, Elena woke at 6 a.m. She automatically began making an elaborate breakfast, just as she had every school day for the past sixteen years. Halfway through cracking eggs for the omelette, no one would eat, so she froze, with a spatula.

"What am I doing?" she whispered to her empty kitchen.

Elena's automatic pilot moment reveals why daily rituals become essential in the empty nest. While weekly templates provide the overall architecture, daily rituals are the interior design that makes your time feel like home. These predictable moments of meaning replace the rhythms previously dictated by your children's needs with patterns you intentionally choose.

David, whose three children left home within two years of each other, described his early empty nest mornings as "untethered."

"I'd been our family's morning coordinator, ensuring everyone had lunches, homework, and the right equipment for after-school activities. Suddenly, my mornings had no guardrails. Some days I'd be productive by 7 a.m., others I'd find myself still in pyjamas at noon, scrolling mindlessly through social media."

David's solution came from an unexpected source—a book on creative habits he'd bought years earlier but never read. "I learned that most successful writers have morning rituals that signal to their brains it's time to work. I decided to design my morning signal system."

His simple ritual now includes making pour-over coffee with the same careful attention each day, spending fifteen minutes journaling, and taking a brief walk around his neighbourhood before settling into his first scheduled activity. "Nothing complicated," he explained, "but the consistency transforms my relationship with mornings. These small acts of intention create a framework that the rest of my day builds upon."

Effective daily rituals share three key characteristics:

1. **Consistency** – They occur at roughly the same time each day, creating a dependable structure
2. **Intentionality** – They serve a specific purpose aligned with your values and goals
3. **Mindfulness** – They're performed with awareness rather than autopilot

The most powerful rituals often frame your day, morning routines that launch your day with purpose and evening rituals that provide meaningful closure.

Morning Ritual Blueprint

Your morning ritual sets the tone for everything that follows. An effective morning ritual includes:

- A **centring practice** to ground yourself before external demands intrude

Examples: Meditation, journaling, prayer, contemplative reading

"I start each day with twenty minutes of meditation followed by brief journaling," Maria said eighteen months into her empty nest journey. "During my parenting years, my mind was filled with everyone else's needs from the moment I woke up. This centring time reclaims my mornings for myself."

- A **physical component** to energise your body

Examples: Stretching, brief yoga sequence, deliberate breathing, short walk

"My body wakes up much more slowly than my mind," explained James, whose last child left for college two years ago. "Taking ten minutes for gentle stretching changes how I experience the rest of my day—I feel more present in my body than just in my thoughts."

- A **planning element** to clarify priorities and intentions

Examples: Reviewing your calendar, identifying three priorities, and visualising successful outcomes

"I spend five minutes with my planner while enjoying my coffee," said Nicole, a year into her empty nest transition. "I identify the three things that would make today meaningful if completed. This simple practice prevents me from reaching evening wondering where the day went."

Evening Ritual Blueprint

Evening rituals provide closure and transition, helping you process the day and prepare for restorative rest. Effective evening rituals typically include:

- A **reflection practice** to acknowledge accomplishments and insights.

Examples: Journaling, gratitude listing, reviewing completions

"Each evening, I write down three things I accomplished and one thing I learned," shared Thomas, whose empty nest coincided with semi-retirement. "This simple practice helps me see progress even on unproductive days."

- A **preparation element** to reduce morning stress.

Examples: Laying out clothes, reviewing tomorrow's priorities, preparing breakfast items

"I spend ten minutes each evening preparing for tomorrow," explained Rebecca. "During my parenting years, I did this for my children. Now I do it for myself, and it's transformed my relationship with mornings."

- A **wind-down sequence** that signals your brain to prepare for sleep.

Examples: Reading fiction, gentle stretching, herbal tea ritual, electronics curfew

"The biggest change in my empty nest routine is my deliberate bedtime ritual," shared Margaret. "With no children to check on or wait up for, I found myself staying up too late without the natural endpoint of their bedtimes once created. Now I have a three-part sequence—herbal tea, fiction reading, and lavender lotion—that signals my body it's time to rest."

The key is developing rituals that feel nourishing rather than obligatory. Unlike the often exhausting routines of active parenting years, your empty nest rituals should leave you feeling restored rather than depleted.

Balancing Purpose, Relationships, Contribution, and Self-Care

Robert's weekly calendar told a stark story about his transition struggles six months into his empty nest. Without the forced balance that his children's activities once imposed, his schedule had become dominated by work commitments that expanded to fill the void left by parenting duties.

"I keep saying I want more time for my marriage and personal interests," he admitted during our coaching session, "but when I look at where my hours go, it's clear I'm avoiding the things I claim to want."

As we analysed his time allocation, the imbalance became obvious:

- 65% devoted to work (including unnecessary overtime and weekend projects)
- 15% spent on basic household management and errands
- 12% allocated to passive entertainment (primarily television)
- 8% invested in his marriage and friendships
- 0% dedicated to community contribution or structured self-care

"When I see these percentages, I hardly recognise myself," Robert confessed. "This isn't the post-parenting life I imagined. I'm using work to avoid the space instead of filling it with things that matter to me."

Robert's situation highlights why intentional balance across life domains becomes essential in the empty nest years. Without the structured variety that children's needs once provided, many empty nesters default to overinvesting in familiar areas while neglecting domains that require new skills or trigger uncertainty.

True time architecture mastery requires thoughtful allocation across four essential domains:

1. **Purpose** – Activities that generate meaning, growth, and achievement

Examples: Career development, creative projects, learning new skills, and building a business

"I realised I needed multiple purpose areas, not just one," explained Sandra, two years into her empty nest. "Now I divide my time between my consulting business, pottery studio practice, and master gardener training. Having various sources of meaningful work has been my salvation."

2. **Relationships** – Investment in connections with spouse, family, friends, and community

Examples: Date nights, friend gatherings, meaningful conversations, family traditions

"The biggest surprise of my empty nest has been how much active attention my marriage needed," shared Michael. "Without kids, creating forced togetherness and shared projects, we had to rebuild our connection as a couple intentionally. Now we protect our relationship time as fiercely as we once guarded our children's activities."

3. **Contribution** – Opportunities to share wisdom and create a positive impact

Examples: Mentoring, volunteering, community service, wisdom sharing

"Finding the right contribution outlet took time," admitted Patricia, whose youngest left three years ago. "I tried three volunteer positions before finding one that utilised my skills while meeting genuine needs. Now my Wednesday volunteer shift is the anchor of my week."

4. **Self-Care** – Practices that maintain physical, emotional, and spiritual well-being

Examples: Exercise, proper nutrition, adequate sleep, stress management, spiritual practices

"During my parenting years, self-care always fell to the bottom of my list," confessed Thomas. "Now I've finally learned that maintaining my wellbeing isn't selfish—it's the foundation everything else depends on. My non-negotiable self-care blocks are now the framework I build my week around."

The proportions will vary based on your circumstances and priorities, but the critical insight is that all four domains require regular attention. This balanced approach prevents the common empty nest traps of becoming entirely self-focused or continuing to over-function for others while neglecting personal renewal.

The Four-Domain Audit
To assess your current balance, conduct a simple time audit using this process:

1. Track where your time goes for one typical week.
2. Categorise each activity within the four domains.
3. Calculate the percentage of time devoted to each domain.
4. Compare your actual allocation with your intended priorities.

"The time audit was a brutal wake-up call," admitted Jennifer, eight months into her empty nest. "I discovered I was spending 70% of my discretionary time on household tasks and administrative details that didn't require that level of attention. I was using busywork to avoid the more meaningful but challenging task of rebuilding my identity."

Many empty nesters discover similar misalignments between stated values and actual time investment. This awareness enables intentional recalibration through specific adjustments to your weekly template and daily rituals.

Designing Energising Rather Than Restrictive Routines
Within three weeks of becoming an empty nester, Diane abandoned the elaborate schedule she'd created with such hope and enthusiasm.

"I'd colour-coded every hour," she explained during our coaching session. "Fitness classes, volunteer commitments, home projects, friend meetups—all carefully arranged to maximise productivity and eliminate space."

She pulled out her abandoned planner, filled with crossed-out appointments and abandoned plans. "It felt like I'd created another job for myself," she continued. "I'd escaped one set of obligations only to create new ones that felt equally suffocating. The whole system collapsed under its weight."

Diane's experience reveals a crucial distinction between restrictive routines that deplete energy and energising structures that generate anticipation. Many empty nesters mistakenly recreate the rigid patterns of their parenting years rather than designing systems aligned with their newfound freedom to choose.

The difference between energising and restrictive time structures emerges from three key factors:

1. **Motivation source** – Energising routines stem from internal desire rather than external obligation

"I realised I was still approaching my schedule with a 'should' mentality," explained Thomas, fourteen months into his empty nest journey. "When I shifted to asking what I genuinely wanted to do rather than what I thought I should do, my resistance to structure disappeared."

2. **Flexibility level** – Energising routines include built-in adaptation points rather than rigid requirements.

"My breakthrough came when I started thinking of my schedule as a living document rather than a set of commands," shared Maria. "I now build in formal decision points where I can adjust based on what's happening rather than what I predicted would work."

3. **Energy management** – Energising routines recognise energy fluctuations rather than demanding constant output.

"During my parenting years, I pushed through regardless of my energy level —the kids needed what they needed when they needed it," recalled James. "Now I've learned to match activities to my natural energy cycles, scheduling creative work for my morning peak and administrative tasks for afternoon lulls."

This shift requires moving beyond traditional time management (focusing solely on how hours are allocated) to embrace energy management (recognising when you have the physical, emotional, and mental resources for different activities).

The Permission Pause Technique

Carol, a recently retired teacher and new empty nester, developed a simple practice that transformed her relationship with time. Before transitioning to each new activity in her day, she pauses briefly to check in with herself:

1. "What is my current energy level?" (physical, emotional, mental)
2. "Does this planned activity align with my current capacity?"
3. "What minor adjustment would make this more energising?"

"I'd spent decades following bell schedules and curriculum timelines," she reflected. "Learning to pause and check in with myself before moving to the next activity felt revolutionary. Sometimes I stick with my original plan, but I often make small adjustments based on what I need."

This simple practice prevents the common empty nest trap of mechanically moving through your day without the responsiveness that true freedom allows. Rather than abandoning structure entirely, permission pauses allow for thoughtful adaptation within your overall architecture.

"The most surprising outcome has been how much more I accomplish," Carol continued. "By honouring my energy patterns rather than forcing myself through a rigid schedule, I complete more meaningful work with less effort. The permission to adjust doesn't lead to laziness—it leads to sustainability."

This approach transforms routines from rigid requirements to supportive frameworks that enhance rather than restrict your newfound freedom.

Key Takeaway

Your time architecture should provide direction without restriction, balancing structure with spontaneity. Creating flexible templates, establishing meaningful rituals, balancing essential life domains, and designing energising routines will transform the formless void of unstructured time into an intentional canvas for your next chapter. Remember that you're not managing time—you're designing it as the architect of your empty nest freedom.

As Rachel—the woman we met at the beginning of this chapter—discovered: "Time used to be my enemy—either too scarce during the busy parenting years or too abundant and formless after my children left. Learning to architect my time rather than react to it has been the key to finding purpose and joy in this new chapter."

As you master the art of time architecture, you'll be prepared to address one of the most meaningful opportunities of your empty nest years—creating a legacy beyond your immediate family. In the next chapter, we'll explore how to design your legacy project, transmitting your wisdom and values in ways that create a lasting impact without overstepping boundaries.

Chapter 14

YOUR LEGACY PROJECT

THE manila envelope sat untouched on Eleanor's desk for three weeks after her youngest left for college.

Inside were the handwritten letters she'd composed during sleepless nights throughout her parenting journey—wisdom she'd planned to share someday. Now, with her children gone, she wondered if that someday had passed. Had she missed her chance to pass on what mattered most? Or could this empty nest phase offer the perfect opportunity to thoughtfully craft her legacy in ways her busy parenting years never allowed?

Eleanor's situation mirrors what many of us face as empty nesters. We've accumulated decades of wisdom through parenting—insights that feel too valuable to fade away with our daily caregiving role. Yet we hesitate, uncertain how to share this wisdom without overstepping boundaries or clinging to our former identity. This chapter will guide you through transforming your parenting wisdom into a meaningful legacy that respects boundaries while creating a lasting impact.

Identifying Your Most Important Wisdom and Values

Sarah stood in her daughter's empty bedroom, fingers tracing the growth chart marked on the wall. Twenty-three years of parenting concentrated into fading pencil marks. "What mattered most?" she wondered. "What wisdom made a difference?"

This question faces every empty nester. After decades of parenting, you've accumulated thousands of insights—from bedtime routines to college applications, from handling playground disputes to navigating teenage heartbreak. Yet not all wisdom carries equal weight. Some lessons fundamentally shaped your children's character, while others, though important at the time, had less lasting impact.

Your legacy project begins by identifying the teachings that truly matter—the wisdom worth preserving and sharing. This process isn't just about what you want to say; it's about what others need to hear.

Start by asking yourself these questions:

1. **What principles guided your parenting decisions during crucial moments?** Think about turning points where your values determined your actions.
2. **Which values did you consistently try to demonstrate, not just teach?** Children learn more from what we do than what we say.
3. **What lessons did you learn too late that could benefit others earlier?** Your mistakes often yield the most valuable wisdom.
4. **What unique perspective did you bring to parenting that differs from conventional wisdom?** Your distinct approach may be your most valuable contribution.
5. **Which insights have your adult children implemented in their own lives?** This reveals what truly resonated with them.

When Martin, a father of three grown sons, tackled these questions, he was surprised by his answers. The elaborate financial lessons he'd carefully planned had made little impact. But his consistent approach to apologising after mistakes—acknowledging error, accepting responsibility, and making amends—had shaped how all three sons handled conflict in their adult relationships. This discovery focused his legacy project on authentic accountability rather than financial management.

The Wisdom Worth Sharing Assessment

Type of Wisdom	Questions to Ask	Examples from Your Experience
Practical Skills	What capabilities did I teach that created genuine independence?	
Relationship Insights	What relationship patterns did I identify that could help others?	

Emotional Intelligence	What emotional lessons took me years to learn?	
Value Systems	What principles consistently guided my decisions?	
Life Strategies	What approaches to life served my family well?	

Take time to complete this assessment, focusing on wisdom that created a meaningful impact. You'll capture your examples in the right column—the specific situations where your wisdom made a difference.

Many empty nesters make the mistake of trying to preserve everything. Judith, a retired teacher and mother of three, initially listed forty "essential" life lessons for her legacy project. After completing this assessment, she narrowed it to five core teachings that had demonstrably impacted her adult children's lives. This focused approach made her legacy more powerful, concentrated rather than diluted.

You've earned the right to be selective. The most meaningful legacy isn't created through quantity but through identifying the wisdom that truly matters. Permit yourself to focus on quality over comprehensiveness.

Selecting Creative Formats for Legacy Transmission
"They'll never read it," Michael said, tossing the manuscript of his unfinished memoir onto his desk. Six months into retirement, the former construction manager had diligently documented his life lessons, but his adult children showed little interest in the growing stack of pages.

Then his daughter visited with her new phone. "Dad, have you seen these short videos everyone's making? You should discuss that bridge project with the impossible deadline."

Michael was sceptical but agreed to a five-minute recording. He described the project challenge and the principle that saved it: "Solve problems at their source, not at their symptom." His daughter posted it to the family's private group. By evening, both sons had watched and commented.

"Tell the one about the foundation crack next," his youngest son requested.

Within weeks, Michael's "Building Wisdom" series had become family favourites, regularly quoted at gatherings. The format transformed everything —the same wisdom that sat unread on paper now sparked family conversations.

The way wisdom is packaged dramatically affects how it's received. The most profound insights can be ignored if presented in formats that don't resonate with your intended audience. Your format selection should align with three criteria:

1. **Your natural communication strengths**
2. **Your recipients' preferred ways of receiving information**
3. **The type of wisdom you're trying to transmit**

Consider these format options for your legacy project:

Written Formats:
- **Family Cookbook with Story Interludes** – Recipes paired with the life lessons or family stories connected to each dish.
- **Letters to Future Generations** – Structured correspondence addressing specific life situations future family members might face.
- **Wisdom Journal** – Topically organised collection of short reflections on specific life domains
- **Question & Answer Book** – Your thoughtful responses to life's most important questions

Visual and Audio Formats:
- **Video or Audio Interviews** – Recorded conversations about specific life experiences and the wisdom gained.
- **Photo Essay Collections** – Images paired with written reflections on the values or insights each represents.
- **Physical Memory Boxes** – Curated collections of meaningful objects with accompanying stories
- **Illustrated Life Principles** – Simple drawings or graphics that capture core values visually.

Interactive Formats:
- **Family Games** – Custom-designed activities that teach family values through play.
- **Ritual Creation** – Developing meaningful family rituals that embody your values.

- **Mentorship Programs** – Structured guidance for specific skills you've mastered.
- **Legacy Projects** – Collaborative family initiatives that apply your wisdom to community needs.

The most effective legacy projects often combine formats. A former teacher, Diana, created a "grandparents' wisdom journal" with written entries. She also included QR codes linking to short videos of her demonstrating specific skills, from making her famous dinner rolls to handling difficult conversations.

The Format Selection Matrix

Format Type	Your Comfort Level (1-10)	Recipient Preference (1-10)	Likelihood of Engagement (1-10)	Total Score
Written	[score]	[score]	[score]	[total]
Visual	[score]	[score]	[score]	[total]
Interactive	[score]	[score]	[score]	[total]

Complete this matrix for each specific format you're considering. The highest scores represent the formats most likely to transmit your wisdom successfully.

When selecting formats, remember that your legacy project should be sustainable. Choose approaches you can realistically maintain given your time, resources, and energy levels. A modest project that's completed has infinitely more impact than an ambitious one that's abandoned. You can start small and let your legacy project grow organically over time.

Sharing Wisdom Without Overstepping Boundaries

Elena sat alone at the restaurant table, stirring her tea while fighting back tears. Her lunch with her newly married daughter had ended abruptly after Elena offered unsolicited advice about managing household finances. "Mom, we need to figure things out ourselves," her daughter had said before leaving. "It feels like you don't trust me to make my own decisions."

The boundary between sharing wisdom and imposing it challenges most empty nesters. You possess valuable insights gained through decades of experience, yet sharing this wisdom often triggers resistance rather than appreciation. This rejection feels personal, as though your life experience is being dismissed.

The boundary challenge stems from how wisdom is shared, not the wisdom itself. Elena had valuable financial insights, but her approach to sharing them

—direct advice without invitation—created resistance. Three months later, she tried a different approach. When her daughter mentioned budgeting struggles, Elena asked, "Would it help to hear how your dad and I handled similar challenges early in our marriage?" The conversation that followed created a genuine connection rather than tension.

Consider these approaches for sharing without overstepping:

- **The Narrative Offering Method**
    - Share wisdom as personal stories rather than direct advice.
    - Begin with "One thing I discovered…" rather than "You should…"
    - Emphasise what worked for you without suggesting it's universal.

- **The Permission-First Approach**
    - Explicitly request permission before sharing insights.
    - Use phrases like "I have some thoughts on this if you're interested".
    - Respect declined invitations without taking offence.

- **The Question-Based Method**
    - Frame wisdom as thoughtful questions rather than statements.
    - Ask "What factors are you considering?" instead of providing solutions.
    - Use "What helped me was…" followed by your experience.

- **The Shared Resource Technique**
    - Offer wisdom through books, articles or resources rather than direct advice.
    - Present options with "This helped me think through similar situations".
    - Create distance between your opinion and the wisdom being shared.

These approaches transform how your wisdom is received. Instead of creating resistance, they invite engagement. The shift might seem subtle, but the impact is profound. One adult child explained, "When my mom tells me what to do, I resist. When she shares her experience, I listen."

Boundary-Respecting Language Conversions

Instead of Saying...	Try This Instead...
"You need to..."	"What worked for me was..."
"The right way to handle this is..."	"I found one approach that helped me was..."
"You're making a mistake by..."	"I made a similar choice once and learned..."
"Let me tell you what to do..."	"Would you be interested in hearing my experience?"
"You should consider..."	"Have you thought about...?"
"If I were you..."	"Everyone's situation is different, but in my case..."

Grace, a mother of four adult children, created an innovative approach for her legacy project. She compiled a list of topics where she had substantial insights, then shared it with her family. They could ask her thoughts on specific subjects relevant to their lives. This "wisdom request system" ensured her insights were both wanted and timely, offered when needed rather than imposed when unwelcome.

The most respectful legacy projects operate on a "pull" rather than "push" model—making wisdom available rather than imposing it. This approach honours your insights and others' boundaries, creating the conditions for genuine wisdom transmission rather than resistance.

Extending Legacy Beyond Your Immediate Family

Robert closed his laptop with a sigh of satisfaction. He'd just finished his weekly email to the community youth coaches he mentored. He'd coached his sons' baseball teams for fifteen years, developing an approach that emphasised character development over competition. When his youngest graduated from high school, Robert assumed his coaching days were over.

Then came the phone call from a parent who remembered Robert's coaching style. "The league needs more coaches like you," she said. "Would you consider sharing your approach with new coaches?"

That conversation launched Robert's legacy project. He developed a community coaching workshop that has trained over fifty local coaches, impacting hundreds of children. "My sons are grown," Robert reflected, "but my coaching philosophy continues to shape young lives. That's a legacy that matters."

Your wisdom has value beyond your biological family. The transition architect mindset invites you to consider how your parenting insights might benefit broader communities. This extension creates three significant benefits:

1. **Expanded Impact** – Your wisdom reaches more people who might benefit from it.
2. **Continued Purpose** – You maintain a meaningful contribution role beyond active parenting.
3. **Enhanced Skill Recognition** – You acknowledge the transferable expertise you've developed.

Consider these avenues for extending your legacy:

- **Mentorship Programs** – Formal or informal guidance for younger parents or professionals.
- **Community Workshops** – Educational sessions on specific parenting or life skills you've mastered.
- **Support Groups** – Facilitated gatherings for those facing challenges you've navigated.
- **Written Resources** – Books, blogs, or articles sharing your insights with broader audiences.
- **Digital Content Creation** – Videos, podcasts, or social media sharing wisdom in accessible formats.
- **Volunteer Consulting** – Offering your expertise to organisations serving families.
- **Intergenerational Initiatives** – Programs connecting older and younger community members.
- **Educational Partnerships** – Collaborations with schools or youth organisations.

Barbara's story exemplifies the potential of extended legacy projects. The former PTA president and mother of three felt adrift after her youngest left for college. Reflecting on her parenting journey, she realised that navigating community resources had been one of her most significant challenges as a new parent. This insight inspired her to create a "New Parent Navigation" program at her local community centre, helping first-time parents connect with community services and support systems. What began as a small project now serves over a hundred families annually.

"I was looking for a way to make my empty nest years meaningful," Barbara explained. "Helping new parents avoid the isolation I experienced gives me purpose while honouring my parenting journey."

When extending your legacy, start with modest, sustainable initiatives rather than ambitious programs that might overwhelm you. The most impactful extended legacies often begin as small projects that grow organically as they demonstrate value.

Many empty nesters worry about presuming expertise. Remember that your wisdom doesn't need to be universal or perfect to be valuable. Your specific experiences, even with their limitations, may provide exactly the perspective someone else needs.

The most meaningful legacy projects combine depth with breadth, offering your most valuable insights to those most likely to benefit from them, whether family members or community connections.

As you develop your legacy project, remember that you're not just preserving the past but actively shaping the future. The wisdom you share becomes part of others' foundations, influencing decisions and perspectives long after you've shared it. This continuation of impact represents the ultimate expression of your transition architect identity—designing meaningful structures that endure beyond your direct involvement.

Your legacy project completes the entitlement foundation we established in the previous chapter. By claiming the validity of your wisdom and designing thoughtful ways to share it, you assert your right to continued significance beyond your daily caregiving role. This assertion isn't about clinging to your parenting identity but about recognising the transferable wisdom you've developed.

In our next chapter, we'll explore how to apply your permission framework to professional reinvention, whether returning to work, changing careers, or starting a business. You'll discover how your transition architect identity creates unique advantages in professional settings, allowing you to leverage decades of parenting experience in new and fulfilling ways.

Chapter 15

PERMISSION IN PROFESSIONAL REINVENTION

The business card sat untouched in the desk drawer for three months. Sarah had ordered it on a whim—a moment of unusual boldness after her youngest left for college. "Sarah Richardson, Marketing Consultant", it proclaimed in elegant serif font. Each morning, she would slide open the drawer, touch the embossed lettering, then close it again without removing a single card. "Not today," she would whisper. "I'm not ready yet." But she meant: "I don't have permission yet."

The business cards represented something far more significant than a potential career. They symbolised an identity Sarah had carefully packed away eighteen years ago when she stepped away from her rising marketing career to focus on raising her children. Now, with an empty nest and decades of potential working years ahead, that identity called to her, but the permission to answer that call seemed perpetually out of reach.

Sarah's story mirrors the experience of countless empty nesters standing at the threshold of professional reinvention. The permission deficit that affects all areas of empty nest life becomes particularly acute in the professional domain, where external validation and credentials seem to matter more than internal authorisation.

When Career Dreams Collide with Permission Barriers
"I remember sitting in the car outside a networking event for nearly forty minutes," Sarah confessed during our interview. "I kept rehearsing what I would say when people asked what I'd been doing for eighteen years. Every explanation I practised sounded like an apology."

This moment, frozen in indecision between your past and future professional selves, is where permission work becomes crucial. The GRANT framework you've built throughout this book offers a systematic path through the permission barriers blocking your professional reinvention.

Before we trace Sarah's journey through each step of the framework, let's acknowledge a truth that research consistently confirms. Still, our culture rarely recognises that your years of intensive parenting have built professional capabilities that many younger workers don't possess. A 2023 LinkedIn workplace study found that recruiters consistently undervalued parenting experience, while managers rated parents who returned to work as having superior skills in crisis management, multitasking, negotiation, and emotional intelligence compared to peers who had remained continuously employed.

The challenge isn't your capabilities—it's your permission to claim them.

Ground: Sarah Establishes Her Professional Foundation
Sarah's journey toward professional reinvention began not with updating her LinkedIn profile or joining networking groups, but with something much more fundamental: granting herself basic permission to want a career again.

"My first assignment seemed almost too simple," Sarah recalled. "I had to write down three statements permitting myself to pursue work that excited me. It took an entire weekend to craft those three sentences. I kept adding qualifiers —' I permit myself to work as long as I'm still available when my kids need me' or 'I grant myself permission to pursue part-time opportunities that don't disrupt family routines.'"

After multiple attempts, Sarah finally created three unqualified professional permission statements:

1. "I give myself permission to pursue work that fully engages my talents and interests."
2. "I grant myself authorisation to invest time and money in rebuilding my marketing career."
3. "I give myself permission to prioritise professional goals alongside family needs."

She wrote these statements on index cards and placed them beside her untouched business cards. She read them aloud each morning before starting her day, gradually establishing the psychological foundation required for the next steps.

This grounding phase also included creating a Professional Permission Inventory—documenting small ways she had already begun granting herself work-related permissions:

- Mentioning her marketing background at her daughter's college orientation
- Subscribing to three industry newsletters
- Updating her ancient LinkedIn profile
- Discussing potential consulting ideas with her husband

"Seeing this list in writing was surprisingly powerful," Sarah noted. "It showed me I'd already started the process, even unconsciously."

Reclaim: Small Professional Steps Build Sarah's Permission Muscle

With her foundation established, Sarah began taking small, low-risk professional actions while practising explicit permission language before each one:

"I give myself permission to attend this marketing webinar without feeling guilty about the time it takes."

"I grant myself authorisation to reach out to my former colleague without apologising for my career gap."

"I give myself full permission to update my skills through this online course, investing time and money in my professional development."

Each action was carefully chosen to build her permission muscle without triggering overwhelming guilt or fear. She documented her emotional responses after each activity:

Professional Action	Permission Statement	Emotional Response
Attended a digital marketing webinar	"I allow myself to invest 2 hours in my professional development."	Initial anxiety about household tasks being delayed; sense of excitement and engagement during webinar; slight guilt afterwards
Coffee with a former colleague	"I grant myself permission to reconnect professionally without diminishing my parenting years."	Nervousness before, surprise at how easily conversation flowed, pride in articulating my current goals

Created a dedicated workspace	"I authorise myself to claim physical space in our home for my professional identity."	Resistance from family members, satisfaction in setting boundaries, and increased focus when working in a dedicated space
Joined the industry Facebook group	"I give myself permission to identify publicly as a marketing professional."	Imposter syndrome when reading others' posts; gradual increase in confidence when participating in discussions
Applied for free industry certification	"I grant myself permission to pursue credentials that validate my capabilities."	Fear of failure, worry about time commitment, and pride in taking concrete steps toward goals.

"The most surprising outcome was how these small actions changed how I spoke about myself," Sarah reflected. "At a dinner party, someone asked what I did, and without thinking, I said 'I'm a marketing consultant' instead of my usual 'I'm just a mom.' The words came out before I could censor them, and they felt right."

Those business cards finally emerged from the drawer.

Amplify: Sarah Expands to Significant Professional Actions

As her permission muscle strengthened, Sarah escalated to more substantial career moves. Each required stronger permission statements and greater boundary-setting:

"I grant myself complete permission to pursue the contract position at MarketWise, recognising that my family can adapt to my professional schedule."

"I authorise myself to invest $2,000 in the digital marketing certification program as an essential foundation for my consulting business."

"I give myself full permission to attend the three-day marketing conference, even though it means missing my son's brief weekend visit home."

These amplified permissions pushed against more profound guilt triggers and required more robust authorisation. For the conference decision, Sarah created a formal half-day "Permission Retreat" where she:

1. Documented the benefits of conference attendance for her long-term goals
2. Listed ways her son's independence would be supported by her professional example
3. Drafted scripts for communicating her decision confidently

4. Created a visualisation of herself confidently networking at the event

"What made this phase different was that I began setting boundaries not just with myself, but with others," Sarah explained. "When my daughter called with a minor crisis during my certification exam, I didn't abandon the test to solve her problem. Instead, I texted that I'd call back in two hours and trusted her to handle it—something that would have been unthinkable six months earlier."

Sarah's amplification phase culminated in her first paid consulting project—a small social media campaign for a local business. Despite her years away from the field, the project required her to present herself as an expert.

"I found myself in a client meeting, speaking confidently about marketing strategies, when a wave of impostor syndrome hit. The client asked about my recent work experience, and I felt that familiar urge to apologise for my 'gap years.' Instead, I took a deep breath and said: 'My background combines traditional marketing expertise with eighteen years of intensive consumer psychology study from the most demanding clients you'll ever meet—teenagers. I bring unique insight into reaching resistant audiences.'"

The client smiled and nodded. The contract was signed the next day.

Normalise: Creating Professional Permission Habits

For Sarah's professional reinvention to sustain itself, she needed to transform conscious permission-granting into automatic habits. She established:

Morning Professional Ritual: Before daily family responsibilities, Sarah spent 15 minutes at her desk reviewing her goals and affirming her professional identity: "I am a skilled marketing consultant entitled to build a thriving business."

Environmental Permission Triggers: She transformed her workspace with visual cues that reinforced her professional authorisation:

- Framed her business license
- Created a wall of client testimonials
- Posted her certification prominently
- Established a "Do Not Disturb" sign that family members respected during client calls

Rapid Response Scripts: She developed automatic responses to everyday permission-eroding situations:

- When family interrupted work: "I'm working now and will be available at 3 pm."
- When feeling guilty about missed family events: "My professional engagement benefits our family both financially and by modelling career fulfilment."
- When clients questioned her experience: "My unique career path provides fresh perspectives alongside proven expertise."

Weekly Professional Development Block: Every Thursday afternoon became a non-negotiable time for industry reading, skills updates, and networking, protected with the same commitment she once gave to her children's activities.

"The normalisation phase was when others began treating my work as real," Sarah noted. "My husband stopped asking if he could interrupt my work calls. My kids started scheduling around my client meetings. Even my mother, who had been sceptical, began introducing me as a marketing consultant rather than just mentioning my children's accomplishments."

Transcend: Sarah Reaches Professional Entitlement

The final step in Sarah's professional permission journey elevated her from needing permission to recognising her inherent entitlement to career fulfilment. This transcendence manifested through:

Professional Declaration of Entitlement: Sarah wrote and framed a formal declaration: "I, Sarah Richardson, am entitled to a fulfilling career that utilises my talents, provides financial rewards, and creates value for clients. This entitlement is my fundamental right to professional expression without qualification or apology."

Visualisation Practice: Each week, Sarah spent time visualising herself as an established professional, conducting workshops, speaking at industry events, and confidently commanding premium rates for her expertise.

Entitlement When Challenged: When her mother-in-law made a passing comment about how Sarah's work was "keeping her busy now that the kids are gone," Sarah responded not with justification but with entitled clarity: "My business isn't a hobby to fill time—it's the professional chapter I've been planning and building toward. I'm excited to see how it continues to grow."

Wisdom Sharing: Perhaps most significantly, Sarah began mentoring other returning professionals, sharing her permission journey from a place of earned authority rather than tentative re-entry.

"The moment I knew I'd transcended permission was during contract negotiations with a major client," Sarah shared. "They offered a rate below my standard, and without hesitation, I declined and held firm on my value. There was no internal debate, no guilt about potentially losing the opportunity. I knew what my expertise was worth and felt entitled to require it. When they came back accepting my terms, it confirmed what I already knew—I had moved beyond needing permission to standing in my professional power."

The Permission-Professional Connection: Your Journey

Sarah's story illustrates the power of applying the GRANT framework to professional reinvention, but your journey will follow your unique path. The framework's structure remains consistent, but the specific permissions you need will reflect your particular barriers and aspirations.

Whether you're returning to a previous career after years away, changing fields entirely, scaling up from part-time to full engagement, or launching an entrepreneurial venture, the permission process follows the same progression:

1. **Ground** yourself in basic authorisation to want professional fulfilment
2. **Reclaim** your right to take small career steps without guilt
3. **Amplify** your permission to make significant professional moves
4. **Normalise** professional self-authorisation through consistent habits
5. **Transcend** to genuine entitlement in your career identity

This progression addresses the core challenge most empty nesters face in professional reinvention: translating intellectual understanding ("I should be allowed to work") into emotional authorisation ("I fully authorise myself to prioritise my career").

The table below will help you identify your specific permission needs based on common professional scenarios:

Professional Scenario	Key Permission Need	Sample Permission Statement
Returning after an extended career break	Permission to claim relevance despite the gap	"I give myself permission to value my current capabilities without apology for my career path."
Career change to a new field	Permission to be a beginner again	"I authorise myself to learn openly, viewing my learner status as an asset rather than a weakness."
Starting a business	Permission to invest resources and take risks	"I grant myself permission to allocate family resources to my business growth with the same priority as other family investments."
Seeking advancement in current role	Permission to prioritise career over availability	"I allow myself to pursue leadership opportunities even when they reduce my family availability."
Scaling back to semi-retirement	Permission to redefine success	"I authorise myself to create a professional identity based on contribution and satisfaction rather than advancement or income."

As you progress through your professional permission journey, remember that the skills you developed during your parenting years translate directly to workplace value:

Parenting Experience	Professional Application
Managing family conflicts	Conflict resolution and mediation
Coordinating complex schedules	Project management and prioritisation
Advocating for children's needs	Client advocacy and relationship management
Handling household finances	Budget management and resource allocation
Teaching children new skills	Training and mentoring capabilities
Navigating school bureaucracies	Organisational politics and system navigation
Crisis management during emergencies	Pressure tolerance and rapid problem-solving
Motivating reluctant children	Leadership and influence without authority
Adapting to children's changing needs	Flexibility and adaptive planning
Maintaining calm during chaos	Emotional intelligence and stress management

Your professional permission journey doesn't end with securing a position or launching a business. Each new career challenge will require fresh permission statements and boundary reinforcement. The difference is that with each successful framework application, your permission muscle strengthens, making future authorisations easier and more automatic.

Remember that your professional reinvention is a powerful model for your adult children. Demonstrating that identity evolution continues throughout life shows them that careers need not be linear, and that reinvention is always possible. Your permission to pursue professional fulfilment ultimately permits them to navigate their career paths with courage and flexibility.

Sarah runs a thriving marketing consultancy with four employees, three years after ordering those business cards. The index cards with her original permission statements remain on her desk—not because she still needs daily authorisation, but as a reminder of the journey from permission to entitlement.

"The cards remind me to extend the same permission to others that I had to fight so hard to give myself," she explained. "Whenever I interview another empty nester for a position, I remember standing outside that networking event, afraid to claim my professional identity. Now I get to be the person who says, 'Your experience matters. Your wisdom is valuable. Your professional chapter is just beginning.'"

In the next chapter, we'll explore how to extend your permission framework to encompass physical well-being, creating sustainable health practices that support your thriving future in an empty nest. The entitled approach to professional reinvention you've developed here will provide a valuable foundation for entitled physical renewal.

Chapter 16

ENTITLED PHYSICAL RENEWAL

ELLEN stood in her doctor's waiting room, a strange feeling of displacement washing over her.

For twenty-three years, she had navigated these medical spaces with her children, holding hands during vaccinations, comforting them through fevers, and advocating for them during diagnoses. Yet in all those years, she rarely sat alone in this room. The receptionist handed her a clipboard with patient forms. Ellen stared at the blank medical history section, suddenly aware of how little attention she had paid to her own physical story while meticulously documenting every sniffle and growth spurt of her three children. Her hand trembled slightly as she checked "unsure" for the date of her last physical examination.

"It's been a while," she whispered, a simple admission that carried the weight of decades of neglect.

Her doctor, a woman about her age, reviewed the sparse form with raised eyebrows. "Ellen, your last comprehensive check-up was nine years ago, just after Jamie's birth. What's brought you in today?"

The question seemed simple enough, but Ellen found herself struggling to come up with an answer. What had brought her in? There was the persistent fatigue she'd attributed to parenting. The occasional chest pain she'd dismissed as stress. The gradually decreasing mobility in her right knee, which she'd accommodated by taking the elevator instead of the stairs. But beyond these specific concerns was something more fundamental—a dawning recognition that her body had become foreign territory, a neglected landscape she'd stopped exploring years ago.

"My youngest left for university last month," Ellen finally said. "And I realised I need to figure out who I am now. Starting with this body that's carried me through motherhood."

The doctor nodded, understanding immediately. "You'd be surprised how often I hear some version of that statement. Let's see where we're starting from."

This chapter isn't about pursuing unrealistic aesthetic ideals or turning back the clock on the natural ageing process. It's about reclaiming what rightfully belongs to you: the entitled care of the vessel that will carry you through your next chapter. The transformation awaiting you isn't just physical—it's a fundamental shift from seeing self-care as an occasional luxury you must apologise for to recognising it as the essential foundation for everything else you hope to create in your empty nest years.

Moving from Neglected Health to Entitled Self-Care
Mark the date on your calendar—today marks a significant turning point in your relationship with your physical self.

Patricia's date was October 17th, three weeks after her youngest daughter moved across the country for graduate school. She sat in her quiet kitchen, absentmindedly rubbing her wrist, which had been aching for months. Her husband walked in and paused, watching her.

"Why don't you finally get that checked out?" he asked. "You've been favouring that wrist since Christmas."

Patricia started to reply with her usual dismissal—it wasn't that bad, she'd get to it eventually, there were more important things to worry about—when a new thought struck her with unexpected force: Who was she saving her health for? What exactly was she waiting for? With her children launched and thriving, what possible reason could justify continuing to place herself last on her priority list?

The next morning, she made three appointments she'd been postponing: a wrist evaluation, an overdue mammogram, and a consultation with a nutritionist. As she marked these in her previously child-centred calendar, she felt something shift inside her—not guilt, as she had expected, but a quiet certainty that she was finally doing what she should have been doing all along.

Health neglect during intensive parenting follows predictable patterns, creating a deficit that accumulates silently until it can no longer be ignored. Research shows that parents—especially mothers—delay an average of 40% of recommended preventive care during active child-raising years. This includes skipping annual check-ups, ignoring screening guidelines, and postponing treatment for non-emergency conditions.

Take a moment now to create your personal "Health Neglect Inventory" by answering these questions:

1. **Medical appointments**: Which recommended check-ups or screenings have you postponed or skipped entirely?
2. **Sleep patterns**: How has your sleep quality and quantity been compromised during parenting years?
3. **Nutrition habits**: In what ways have your eating patterns been shaped around family preferences rather than your own needs?
4. **Movement patterns**: How has regular physical activity been sacrificed to accommodate others' schedules?
5. **Stress management**: What techniques for managing stress have you abandoned due to time constraints?

Area of Neglect	Common Parenting Pattern	Empty Nest Opportunity
Preventive Care	Skipping annual physicals and screenings	Schedule a comprehensive health assessment
Sleep	Interrupted sleep patterns, chronic sleep debt	Establish a consistent sleep routine
Nutrition	Eating children's leftovers, meal planning around others' preferences	Design eating patterns around personal needs
Physical Activity	Abandoning personal exercise for children's activities	Rediscover enjoyable movement practices
Stress Management	No time for relaxation practices	Implement daily stress reduction techniques

Rachel, a 56-year-old former marketing executive and mother of two, described her mindset shift this way: "I used to think taking care of myself was something I had to squeeze in if everything else was handled first. Now I view it completely differently—my well-being is the foundation that makes everything else possible. If I'm depleted, I have nothing meaningful to offer anyone, including my adult children."

This perspective transforms self-care from a selfish indulgence to a responsible necessity. When you board an aeroplane, flight attendants instruct you to put on your oxygen mask before helping others, not because you matter more, but because you cannot effectively help if you're deprived of oxygen, this wisdom applies perfectly to your empty nest years: your physical well-being must become your priority, not your last.

The permission statement that launched Rachel's transformation can also launch yours: "I fully authorise myself to prioritise my physical well-being without apology or explanation."

Creating Sustainable Fitness Routines Without Guilt
Daniel stood at the edge of the community pool, watching swimmers glide through the water with an ease that seemed impossible to him.

At 58, he couldn't remember the last time he'd exercised deliberately. Sure, he'd spent years coaching his sons' soccer teams, demonstrating drills and occasionally joining practice games. He'd helped move countless pieces of furniture, carried sleeping children from cars to beds, and tackled home renovation projects. But an actual planned movement for his health? That had disappeared somewhere in the busy years of raising twin boys.

"First time?" asked an older gentleman, towelling off nearby.

Daniel nodded, feeling oddly vulnerable in his new swim shorts. "My doctor suggested swimming might help my back issues. I haven't been in a pool since the boys were little."

The man smiled. "I started at 62 after a heart scare. Could barely make it across the pool once. Now I'm here three mornings a week. My best decision was showing up that first day."

"I'm not sure I remember how to swim properly," Daniel admitted.

"The water will remind you," the man said simply, heading toward the changing room.

Daniel took a deep breath and stepped down the ladder into the pool. The sensation was immediately familiar—not to his parenting self but to some earlier version of himself that had loved the feeling of weightlessness. He pushed off gently from the wall, surprised by how his body seemed to remember what to do. He managed only four laps that first day, but as he drove home, he noticed something surprising: he felt more awake, more present than he had in years.

For many empty nesters, physical movement has become disconnected from joy, associated instead with obligation, punishment, or impossible beauty standards. Years of starting and stopping fitness regimens—interrupted by family needs—have created a cycle of guilt and failure. The key to sustainable movement practices in your empty nest years is completely reimagining your relationship with physical activity.

Begin by discarding these common myths about fitness after 50:

- **Myth**: You must engage in vigorous exercise to see benefits. **Truth**: Even gentle, consistent movement creates significant health improvements.
- **Myth**: You should push through pain to get results. **Truth**: Pain is your body's warning system and should be respected.
- **Myth**: You need to dedicate large time blocks to exercise. **Truth**: Multiple short movement sessions create cumulative benefits.
- **Myth**: The goal of fitness is weight loss or appearance change. **Truth**: Energy, mood improvement, and disease prevention are the most valuable benefits.
- **Myth**: You need special equipment or gym memberships. **Truth**: Simple, home-based movement practices can be highly effective.

The permission pathway for establishing sustainable fitness begins with a single question that Daniel discovered that day at the pool: "What physical activities feel good to my body?"

Martin, a 59-year-old father of two who had been sedentary for decades, found his answer: "I kept trying to force myself to run because that's what I thought 'counted' as exercise. I hated every minute and would quit after a week. My physical therapist suggested I experiment with different movements to find what didn't feel like punishment. I love swimming—the weightlessness, the quiet, the rhythm. I've gone three times weekly for two years because I genuinely look forward to it."

Finding movement that generates energy rather than depletes it transforms exercise from an obligation to a gift. The critical factor isn't intensity but consistency, which only comes from choosing activities you genuinely enjoy.

Your next step is creating a "Movement Menu" that includes:

1. **Daily foundation movements**: Simple activities you can incorporate throughout your day (stretching while kettle boils, walking while on phone calls).

2. **Scheduled activity sessions**: 2-4 weekly appointments with yourself for more focused movement.
3. **Social movement opportunities**: Activities that combine physical movement with social connection.
4. **Indoor backup options**: Movement practices you can do regardless of weather or circumstances.
5. **Adventure explorations**: New physical activities you're curious to try.

When guilt arises—and it will—practice these permission statements:

"I give myself full permission to prioritise movement that supports my well-being." "My physical health directly impacts my ability to be present for others." "This time for physical activity is non-negotiable and does not require justification."

These statements, practised consistently, gradually dismantle the guilt triggers that have sabotaged your self-care efforts for decades.

Addressing Long-Postponed Health Issues

In her car, Sophie sat outside the specialist's office, staring at the appointment card.

The knee pain started over a decade ago when her daughter was in middle school. She'd wrapped it, iced it, swallowed over-the-counter painkillers, and adjusted her life around the growing limitation. No more tennis. No more hiking. No more kneeling to garden. Each accommodation had seemed small at the time, but now, Sophie suddenly recognised how much territory she had surrendered.

"You've been limping for years, Mom," her daughter had said during her last visit home from college. "Aren't you going to do anything about it?"

The question had struck Sophie with unexpected force. What exactly was she waiting for? Permission? For her children to be even more launched? For some magical moment, would addressing her pain finally feel justified?

The specialist confirmed what Sophie had suspected: her condition was treatable. She could regain much of her mobility with proper physical therapy and possibly a minor procedure. "Why did you wait so long to come in?" he asked, reviewing her intake form.

Sophie offered her usual explanation about being busy with the kids, but stopped herself. The truth was more complicated. Somewhere along the way, she had internalised the belief that her physical suffering didn't merit attention —that "good mothers" pushed through pain without complaint, that self-neglect was somehow a badge of parental dedication.

"I think I was waiting to feel entitled to getting better," she said finally. "And I'm not willing to wait anymore."

Medical self-neglect becomes a normalised pattern for many parents, particularly mothers. You may have been living with concerning symptoms for years, dismissing them as "just stress" or "normal ageing." Perhaps you've received a diagnosis but never followed through with recommended treatments because someone else's needs always seemed more pressing. This pattern of minimising your health concerns ends now.

Your first concrete step is scheduling a comprehensive health assessment with practitioners who specialise in midlife health. This typically includes:

- Complete physical examination
- Age-appropriate screenings
- Hormonal evaluation
- Bone density assessment
- Nutritional analysis
- Sleep quality evaluation
- Mental health screening

Michael, a 57-year-old father who had ignored chronic pain for years, shared his experience: "I'd been managing back pain with over-the-counter medication for so long I didn't even think about it anymore. When I finally saw a specialist after my son left for college, I discovered I had a condition that was completely treatable with physical therapy. I suffered needlessly for eight years because I kept putting off taking care of it."

When addressing postponed health issues, many empty nesters encounter unexpected emotional responses. Anger at having neglected yourself for so long. Grief for the suffering that might have been prevented. Fear about what might be discovered. These emotions are normal and deserve acknowledgement.

Your next step is developing a "Health Advocacy Plan" that includes:

1. **Documentation**: Create a comprehensive list of symptoms, concerns, and questions.
2. **Support**: Bring a friend or partner to important appointments for emotional support.
3. **Follow-through**: Establish a system for implementing recommendations.
4. **Financial planning**: Research insurance coverage and create a health investment budget.
5. **Progress tracking**: Monitor improvements to maintain motivation.

Remember: addressing long-postponed health issues isn't selfish—it's the most responsible action you can take for yourself and those who love you.

Developing a Physical Renewal Mindset

Jennifer woke before her alarm, surprised by the unfamiliar sensation flooding her body with energy.

At 53, she had grown so accustomed to persistent fatigue that she'd forgotten what it felt like to wake naturally, feeling rested and ready for the day. Three months into her physical renewal journey, the changes were becoming noticeable. The afternoon crashes had diminished. The brain fog had lifted. Even her persistent digestive issues had improved with the nutritional changes her doctor had recommended.

She slipped out of bed and moved to the mirror, studying her reflection with new eyes. The woman looking back at her wasn't dramatically different on the outside—no magical transformation had occurred. But there was a subtle shift in her posture, the clarity of her gaze, and the way she held herself. For the first time in decades, she looked at her body not as an enemy failing her or a tool that served others, but as her most faithful companion—one deserving of care, respect, and gratitude.

"Thank you," she whispered to her reflection, touching her heart. It began a new morning ritual acknowledging the profound shift in her relationship with her physical self.

Your relationship with your body requires fundamental reconstruction at this life stage. For decades, you've likely viewed your body primarily as a tool for serving others—a vehicle for carpooling, a machine for household maintenance, an instrument for meeting everyone's needs but your own. This perspective, while perhaps necessary during intensive parenting years, will sabotage your empty nest freedom if not transformed.

The entitled physical renewal mindset recognises four essential truths:

1. **Your body is your primary home** for experiencing your next chapter.
2. **Your energy levels directly impact** your capacity for purpose and meaning.
3. **Physical well-being is the foundation** for everything else you hope to create.
4. **Self-care is a responsibility**, not an indulgence.

Jennifer described her mindset transformation: "I used to see my body as this separate thing that was always letting me down—too tired, too achy, too old. Through this work, I've developed a completely different relationship with it. Despite how I've treated it, I now see that my body has been incredibly faithful to me. It's carried me through raising children, building a career, and handling crises. Now it's time for me to be faithful to it in return."

This reciprocal relationship with your physical self forms the core of the entitled renewal mindset.

To develop this mindset for yourself, begin practising these daily affirmations:

- "My physical well-being deserves the same care I've always given others."
- "Taking time for health practices is an investment, not a luxury."
- "My body is not my enemy but my most faithful companion."
- "I am entitled to the energy and vitality needed for my next chapter."
- "Self-care is the foundation that makes all other contributions possible."

The physical renewal mindset extends beyond health practices to encompass your entire relationship with embodiment. Consider how you talk about your body, the clothes you choose, the environments you create, and the boundaries you establish. Each choice either reinforces or undermines your entitled relationship with physical well-being.

This mindset transformation requires consistent practice. You strengthen your entitled physical renewal mindset when prioritising rest when tired, nourishment when hungry, or stiff movement. You reinforce this new relationship each time you speak respectfully about your body rather than criticising it.

The culmination of this work is the profound recognition that your body is not just something you have but something you are. Integrating physical experience with your whole identity creates the foundation for genuine entitlement to well-being that will sustain you through your next chapter.

Chapter 17

FINANCIAL PERMISSION FRAMEWORK

THE credit card felt unusually heavy in Ellen's hand as she stood frozen before the register, a $95 pottery class receipt awaiting her signature.

Ellen had discovered her love for ceramics in college, decades before marriage and motherhood redirected her creative energy toward science fair projects and homemade Halloween costumes. Now, with her youngest at university and her schedule finally her own, she'd spotted the eight-week class advertised at the community centre. Yet as the moment of payment arrived, her hand trembled slightly. "This money could go toward Megan's textbooks next semester," whispered the familiar voice in her head. The fact that Megan had a part-time job and had insisted she could handle her expenses didn't silence the voice. Ellen's finger hovered over the credit card reader as the shop owner waited patiently.

This moment – this seemingly small financial decision – represented everything about the empty nest transition that felt impossible to navigate.

Overcoming Guilt Around Personal Spending

Ellen's struggle mirrors what I've witnessed with hundreds of empty nesters. The financial permission gap often proves more challenging than any actual budget constraint. Your brain has spent decades creating neural pathways that automatically sort expenses into two categories: "necessary" (anything for your children or household) and "selfish" (anything primarily for your enjoyment).

"I stood in Target last week, agonising over a $24 throw pillow for our living room," admitted Rebecca, a marketing executive and mother of two college students, during one of our group sessions. "Meanwhile, I had just ordered $200 worth of dorm supplies for my son without a second thought. It's not about the money but who deserves it."

This deserving calculation lies at the heart of financial permission. Your brain has created a hierarchy where your needs and wants automatically rank below everyone else's. Until you address this hierarchy directly, no amount of budgeting advice will change your spending patterns.

The Financial Autobiography Exercise

Begin by writing a brief financial autobiography focusing on how your spending patterns changed when you became a parent. Most empty nesters identify a clear "before and after" story:

1. What purchases did you regularly make for yourself before children?
2. What was the first significant purchase you remember postponing or cancelling because of your children's needs?
3. What's one thing you've wanted for years but have never "gotten around to" purchasing?

This exercise isn't about judgment or regret—it's about recognition. You made appropriate choices during your active parenting years. The question now is whether those same choices serve this new chapter.

Next, conduct what I call the "Financial Permission Test." Pull out three months of credit card or bank statements and highlight every purchase made exclusively for your enjoyment or fulfilment. These highlights are surprisingly sparse for most empty nesters, even though their financial situation could support more personal spending.

"I was shocked when I did this exercise," shared Michael, a father of three adult daughters. "In three months, I'd spent thousands on home repairs, gifts for my kids, and helping my oldest with a security deposit—but less than $50 on things just for me. And it wasn't because we couldn't afford it."

Creating Your Permission Bridge

The path from financial guilt to entitled spending isn't crossed in a single leap. Instead, you need a "Permission Bridge"—a structured approach to gradually increasing personal spending while processing and releasing the associated guilt.

Week	Permission Level	Action Step	Reflection Question
1	Micro-permission	Make one $15-25 purchase solely for your enjoyment	What physical sensations arose during this purchase?
2	Mini-permission	Allocate $50-75 toward a personal interest or hobby	What thoughts tried to talk you out of this spending?
3	Moderate permission	Invest $100-150 in personal development or self-care	How does this spending connect to your emerging identity?
4	Major permission	Make a significant purchase ($200+) you've been postponing	What does allowing this purchase say about your values?

For each step, use specific permission language before spending: "I give myself permission to spend [amount] on [purchase] because I am worthy of investment." Record your physical and emotional responses in your Permission Journal.

Ellen completed this bridge process with the pottery class serving as her "major permission" in week four. "The first class felt almost illicit," she admitted. "But by the third session, something shifted. I stopped calculating how many of Megan's meals this could cover and felt grateful I could create again."

Rebalancing Financial Priorities After Active Parenting

Thomas and Marta sat at their kitchen table, surrounded by bills and a calculator in hand. Their son's final college tuition payment had been submitted the previous month, ending 15 years of education expenses for their three children. "We should have an extra $1,800 a month now," Thomas noted, looking up from his calculations. "The question is: what happens to that money?"

This financial inflexion point arrives for all parents, though often unnoticed and unplanned. The resources previously directed toward raising children suddenly become available. However, without intentional reallocation, most empty nesters allow lifestyle inflation to absorb these funds without furthering their future goals.

"We never made a conscious decision," said Jennifer, whose youngest had left for college two years earlier. "Somehow, we're spending exactly what we spent before, just on different things. But when I look at where the money's going, it's not supporting the life I want to build now."

The Next Chapter Financial Blueprint

Rather than passively allowing your spending to redistribute itself, create a conscious "Next Chapter Financial Blueprint" that aligns your resources with your emerging identity. This process begins with a comprehensive review of your "Parent-Era Budget" versus your "Architect-Era Budget."

Samantha and David completed this exercise after their twin daughters graduated from college. Their reallocation revealed significant opportunities to fund their next chapter:

Expense Category	Parent-Era (Monthly)	Architect-Era (Monthly)	Difference	Reallocation Plan
Housing	$2,300	$1,800	-$500	Downsized to a smaller home closer to downtown
Children's needs	$1,200	$200	-$1,000	Birthday/holiday gifts and occasional support only
Food/Groceries	$800	$500	-$300	Cooking for two instead of fourteen appetites
Activities/Sports	$400	$0	-$400	No more youth sports or school activities
Family vacations	$400	$0	-$400	Replaced with a couple of travel funds
Total Released			-$2,600	
Retirement savings	$800	$1,500	+$700	Increased 401(k) and Roth IRA contributions
Travel fund	$200	$800	+$600	Monthly auto-transfer to a dedicated account
Personal development	$0	$500	+$500	Classes, workshops, conferences
Health/Fitness	$100	$400	+$300	Gym membership, trainer, and preventive care
Entertainment/Social	$150	$350	+$200	Concerts, dining out, and events with friends
Giving/Legacy	$100	$300	+$200	Supporting causes aligned with values
Total Reallocated			+$2,500	

"Seeing it laid out this way was transformative," Samantha shared. "We weren't actually 'taking' from our family by changing our spending—we were simply allocating resources to the life stage we're actually in, not the one we'd completed."

Complete your blueprint by tracking your current spending for 30 days, categorising expenses, and creating a new allocation reflecting your architect identity. Permission is crucial—you must authorise yourself to divert funds previously dedicated to family needs.

"I had to write out an official permission slip to myself," David laughed. "It sounds silly, but signing that paper giving myself permission to spend $500 monthly on woodworking classes instead of putting it toward the kids somehow made it feel legitimate."

Creating Appropriate Financial Boundaries with Adult Children

The text message arrived just as Patricia booked flights for the Mediterranean cruise she and her husband had delayed for fifteen years while raising their family. "Mom, my roommate bailed, and I'm short $600 for rent this month. Can you help? I promise I'll pay you back!"

Patricia felt her stomach tighten. The cruise deposit of $750 was due today to secure their cabins. Her daughter Rachel, at 24, had encountered similar financial shortfalls every few months since graduation. Patricia and her husband covered the gap each time, postponing their plans. With retirement five years away and their travel dreams repeatedly deferred, Patricia found herself at a crossroads all too familiar to empty nesters.

"The hardest word in English for most empty nesters is that two-letter word: 'no,'" explains financial psychologist Dr. Michelle Torres. "After decades of saying 'yes' to your children's needs, establishing financial boundaries feels like abandonment rather than healthy separation."

This challenge intensifies because financial support represents one of the last tangible ways parents can "parent" their adult children. When everyday caregiving ends, financial assistance becomes the primary remaining avenue for expressing care, making withdrawal psychologically difficult.

The Clear Boundary Framework

When Rachel's text arrived, Patricia used what I call the "Clear Boundary Framework"—a three-step approach to establishing financial boundaries while maintaining supportive relationships:

1. **Acknowledge their situation empathetically**: "That sounds stressful, and I'm sorry you're dealing with this roommate situation."

2. **Communicate your boundary**: "Dad and I aren't able to cover this expense. We've committed to our retirement planning and the travel we've postponed for many years."
3. **Offer alternative support if appropriate**: "I'm happy to help you review your budget to identify areas where you can cut back this month, or brainstorm ways you could earn extra income to cover the gap."

Patricia reported that implementing this framework wasn't easy but proved transformative. "Rachel was upset initially, but later told me it forced her to have a serious conversation with her roommate and create a payment plan. She handled it herself and seemed proud afterwards."

The Support Continuum Model

Another helpful tool is understanding the "Support Continuum" from enabling to empowering. Most parents unconsciously slide toward the enabling end during the empty nest transition, seeking to maintain connection through financial assistance.

Support Type	Description	Example	Effect on Adult Child
Enabling Support	Resolves problems that adult children could solve themselves	Paying their rent when they overspend	Delays financial maturity
Rescuing Support	Steps during non-emergency shortfalls	Covering overdraft fees	Prevents consequences that prompt learning
Supplementing Support	Regularly subsidises lifestyle beyond means	Paying the phone bill, car insurance, and monthly	Creates dependency and entitlement
Investing Support	Provides resources that build capacity	Helping with education, professional development	Increases future independence
Empowering Support	Offers guidance while requiring responsibility	Helping create a budget, but not providing funds	Builds confidence and capability

"I realised I was stuck in 'rescuing' mode," admitted Gerald, father of two sons in their late twenties. "Every time they called with a money issue, I felt this rush of being needed. But I was preventing them from building their financial muscles."

Moving along this continuum requires permission to parent differently, to be temporarily misunderstood, and to prioritise long-term empowerment over short-term harmony. Practice statements like: "I give myself permission to let my adult children experience the natural financial consequences," and "I deserve to allocate my resources toward my financial future."

Entitled Retirement Planning and Wealth Building

Maria had always been diligent about her children's college funds, contributing monthly since their births. Yet her retirement accounts remained minimal. At 56, with her children launched, a financial advisor delivered sobering news: her retirement funds would last roughly seven years at her current rate of savings.

"But I've always been responsible with money," Maria protested, showing the advisor her children's fully funded education accounts.

"You've been responsible for everyone except yourself," the advisor noted gently. "Now it's time to redirect that responsibility."

This conversation plays out frequently in my work with empty nesters. The permission deficit that affects day-to-day spending often has a more severe impact on retirement planning. The long-term nature of retirement saving makes it especially vulnerable to the "everyone else first" mindset that characterises the parenting years.

The Oxygen Mask Principle

Remember the airline safety instructions that advise you to secure your oxygen mask before helping others? This principle applies powerfully to retirement planning. Your financial security isn't selfish—the foundation allows you to be a resource rather than a burden to your family as you age.

William and Catherine attended my workshop after realising they had saved less than $100,000 for retirement at age 60. "We put three kids through college debt-free and helped with down payments on their first homes," William explained. "We don't regret it, but now we're facing working well into our seventies."

I introduced them to the "Retirement Rescue Framework"—a structured approach for those who need to increase retirement security during their final working years rapidly:

1. **Maximise catch-up contributions:** At 50+, you can contribute extra to retirement accounts beyond standard limits ($7,500 additional to 401(k) plans and $1,000 extra to IRAs as of 2023)
2. **Consider working 2-3 years longer than planned:** Each additional year improves retirement finances in three ways: more contribution time, more growth time, and fewer withdrawal years
3. **Downsize housing earlier rather than later:** Moving to a less expensive home can free up equity to invest while reducing ongoing expenses
4. **Develop specific skills that allow part-time work in retirement:** Create income sources that don't require full-time commitment
5. **Practice extreme catch-up saving:** Temporarily living on 50-60% of income to direct maximum resources toward retirement accounts

William and Catherine implemented this framework with remarkable results. "We downsized from our four-bedroom suburban home to a downtown condo, which freed up $275,000 to invest," Catherine shared. "We're working three years longer than originally planned, but we only need to work part-time for the final two years. And we're now saving 45% of our income for retirement."

Their story illustrates the power of entitled retirement planning, authorised by themselves rather than external permission. "The hardest part wasn't the financial changes," William noted. "It was giving ourselves permission to prioritise our future when we'd spent decades prioritising our children's futures."

The Legacy Reframe

For many empty nesters, saving for retirement feels selfish until it is reframed as legacy planning. Consider these perspective shifts:

1. Financial independence protects your children from future caregiving burdens
2. Secure retirement allows you to help grandchildren if desired, rather than requiring help yourself
3. Building wealth creates potential legacy gifts that extend your impact

Maria applied this reframe by creating her "Independence Fund" rather than her "Retirement Fund." "The new name helped me see that I wasn't just saving for vacations—I was preserving my children's freedom from having to support me later."

She committed to working three years longer than planned, downsized to a smaller home, and directed 40% of her income to catch-up retirement contributions. "Every time I transfer money to my Independence Fund, I remind myself: this is a gift to my whole family, not just me."

Financial Permission Integration Practices

As you work to integrate financial permission into your daily life, implement these practices over the next 30 days:

Week 1: Financial Permission Statement Cards. Create small cards with permission statements addressing your specific financial guilt triggers. Place these cards with your credit cards, chequebook, and online banking login. Before any financial decision, read the appropriate statement aloud.

Week 2: Daily Joy Allocation Practice. Allocate $5-10 daily specifically for something that brings you joy. Document both the purchase and your emotional response in your Permission Journal. Notice how the guilt response changes with repetition.

Week 3: Financial Vision Board Create a visual representation of what your entitled financial future looks like—travel destinations, living arrangements, experiences you'll fund. Place this where you'll see it daily as a reminder of why entitled financial planning matters.

Week 4: Financial Freedom Declaration Write a formal declaration of your financial entitlement that includes:

- Acknowledgement of your responsible financial history
- Recognition of your right to prioritise your financial well-being
- Specific commitments to your financial future
- Permission to say no to financial requests that jeopardise these commitments

Sign and date this declaration, then share it with a supportive friend or partner as a witness.

As Maria discovered during her financial transformation, "Money decisions reflect our deepest beliefs about our worth. Each time I authorise myself to invest in my future, I'm not just moving numbers in an account—I'm declaring that my needs matter. That I matter."

Extending your permission framework to financial decisions creates monetary freedom and psychological liberation from decades of prioritising others over yourself. Your relationship with money becomes an expression of your architectural identity rather than a relic of your parent-only identity.

In the next chapter, we'll explore perhaps the most central relationship in your empty nest: your marriage. The "Marriage Renaissance Architecture" chapter will help you design a vibrant partnership that evolves beyond co-parenting into a foundation for mutual growth and shared adventure.

Chapter 18

MARRIAGE RENAISSANCE ARCHITECTURE

Sarah stared at her husband across the breakfast table, realising they hadn't seen each other in years.

The morning after dropping their youngest at college, Sarah and Michael sat in uncomfortable silence, the crossword puzzle between them untouched. Twenty-three years of conversations about soccer schedules, parent-teacher conferences, and college applications had left them speechless now that those topics had vanished. The question hung between them: who were they to each other without their children as the central focus of their relationship? Equally terrifying and full of potential, this moment marks the beginning of the marriage renaissance opportunity.

Your empty nest presents an unprecedented opportunity to reevaluate your partnership. This isn't merely about surviving this transition together—it's about building a more vibrant and connected relationship than you had during your active parenting years.

Rediscovering Your Partnership Beyond Co-parenting

"I don't even know what you like to do anymore," Michael confessed to Sarah that first silent morning.

This candid admission became the first step in their rediscovery journey. Like many couples, they had gradually transformed from passionate partners with shared interests into efficient family managers, coordinating schedules and dividing parental responsibilities. Their relationship hadn't disappeared—it had been buried under years of necessary parenting logistics.

Think of this rediscovery process as relationship archaeology. You're carefully uncovering what initially connected you while building something new that honours your history and who you've become.

Interest Archaeology Exercise
To begin this excavation, complete this exercise independently, then share your discoveries:

1. List three activities you enjoyed together before having children.
2. Identify two conversation topics that energised you both early in your relationship.
3. Name one quality initially attracted you to your partner that you haven't acknowledged recently.

When Sarah and Michael completed this exercise, they rediscovered their shared love of hiking that had been abandoned when weekend sports tournaments became the priority. Their first empty nest trail adventure felt simultaneously familiar and entirely new, connecting them to their past while creating space for fresh conversations about their future.

Permission statement: "I give myself permission to rediscover who we are as a couple beyond our parenting roles, recognising that this exploration strengthens rather than diminishes our family connections."

Value Alignment Conversation
The strongest marriage renaissances happen when couples identify core values that transcend their parenting roles. Use these questions during an uninterrupted dinner conversation:

1. What three values mattered most to you when raising our children?
2. Which of these values remain essential to your identity now?
3. How might we express these values together in this new chapter?

For Michael and Sarah, their shared value of education, previously channelled into their children's development, transformed into a joint commitment to adult literacy programs in their community. This created a meaningful shared purpose, honouring their parenting journey while moving beyond it.

Permission statement: "We give ourselves permission to evolve our expression of shared values beyond how they manifested in our parenting years."

Creating Meaningful Couple Rituals and Experiences

"Monday nights were always Jason's basketball games," Sarah said, staring at their suddenly empty calendar. "What do we do with Monday nights now?"

This question highlights the second challenge of marriage renaissance: creating intentional rituals that rebuild connection. Unlike the externally imposed structure of family life, these practices must be consciously designed and maintained.

Rather than leaving Mondays blank, Sarah and Michael created "Culinary Adventure Night"—taking turns selecting a new recipe to prepare together each week. This simple practice established a consistent connection while acknowledging their newfound exploration freedom.

The ritual architecture matrix helps identify what to keep, modify, or create:

Ritual Category	Former Family Ritual	Couple Adaptation	New Empty Nest Ritual
Daily	Family dinner check-ins	Evening tea and reflection	Morning intention setting
Weekly	Sunday family meetings	Weekend planning breakfast	Saturday exploration day
Monthly	Birthday celebrations	Monthly relationship review	New experience commitment
Yearly	Holiday traditions	Anniversary adventures	Seasonal relationship retreats

All effective relationship rituals share three key elements:

1. **Consistency** - A regular time and basic structure
2. **Meaning** - Connection to your values and relationship vision
3. **Pleasure** - Enjoyment that creates anticipation rather than obligation

Conversation Ritual Design

"I Realise we've been talking about the kids for so long, I'm not sure what else to discuss," Michael admitted one evening, three weeks into their empty nest.

This common challenge emerges because many couples rely almost exclusively on logistical discussions during active parenting years, which doesn't sustain intimacy after children leave. Sarah and Michael designed a new dinner conversation ritual using this framework:

1. **Logistics** (10 minutes) - Handle necessary planning and coordination
2. **Learning** (15 minutes) - Share something new you've discovered or learned
3. **Listening** (20 minutes) - Practice deep attention to one another's experiences
4. **Longing** (15 minutes) - Express hopes, dreams, and desires for your future

The structure felt awkward initially, but within weeks, their conversations flowed naturally between these elements, creating a more profound connection than they'd experienced in years.

Permission statement: "We give ourselves permission to prioritise meaningful connection through intentional rituals, recognising that our relationship deserves the same care we gave to our children's development."

Navigating Differences in Empty Nest Adaptation

"I don't understand why you're not excited about this," Michael said, frustrated after presenting Sarah with brochures for a European trip. "We've talked about travelling for years once the kids were gone."

Sarah sighed. "I know, but I still feel so lost without them. I need time to figure out who I am before planning big adventures."

This exchange illustrates the most significant challenge in marriage renaissance: asynchronous adaptation—when partners adjust to the empty nest at different rates or in various ways. This creates tension precisely when your relationship needs unity.

Michael embraced the empty nest immediately, eager to travel and explore new interests. Sarah felt unmoored without her daily caregiving role and needed time to process her grief before considering new possibilities. Their different adaptation paces created conflict until they recognised that neither approach was wrong, just different.

Adaptation Styles Assessment

Understanding your natural adaptation tendencies fosters compassion during this transition. Identify which pattern matches each partner:

Style	Characteristics	Needs	Challenges
Enthusiastic Explorer	Quickly embraces change, generates many ideas, and seeks new experiences	Freedom to explore, validation for enthusiasm	May appear insensitive to partner's grief
Reflective Processor	Needs time to absorb change, processes emotions before action, seeks meaning	Space for reflection, validation of feelings	May appear stuck or resistant to the partner
Practical Restructurer	Focuses on reorganising daily life, creates new systems and routines	Concrete plans, clear responsibilities	May avoid the emotional aspects of transition
Reluctant Adjuster	Resists acknowledging changes, maintains parent-centred identity	Gradual transition, continued family connection	May impede the partner's adaptation

Michael fit the Enthusiastic Explorer pattern, while Sarah was a Reflective Processor. Recognising these differences helped them stop judging each other's responses and start supporting their journeys.

Permission statement: "We give each other permission to adapt to our empty nest at different paces and in different ways, respecting our processes while remaining connected."

Asynchronous Adaptation Strategies

When you and your partner are moving at different speeds, try these approaches:

1. **Create a transition vocabulary** - Develop shared language to discuss your adaptation process without judgment.
2. **Establish transition check-ins** - Schedule regular conversations about how you're each experiencing the change.
3. **Design parallel activities** - Find ways to simultaneously honour both partners' needs.
4. **Practice adaptation empathy** - Imagine the transition from your partner's perspective.

After understanding their different styles, Michael and Sarah created "Tuesday/Thursday balance"—Tuesdays, Michael joined Sarah in quieter reflection activities, while Thursdays, Sarah participated in Michael's more adventurous plans. This honoured both adaptation styles while maintaining their connection.

"I thought you were rejecting me when you didn't want to make travel plans," Michael admitted during one of their check-ins.

"And I thought you were dismissing my feelings when you kept pushing for big changes," Sarah responded.

This honest exchange marked a turning point in their adaptation, creating space for their journeys.

Permission statement: "I give myself permission to be patient with our different adaptation paces, recognising that our asynchronous adjustment is normal and temporary."

Designing a Shared Vision for Your Next Chapter

Six months into their empty nest, Sarah surprised Michael by spreading magazines, travel brochures, and coloured markers across their dining room table one Saturday morning.

"I'm ready now," she said with a smile. "Let's design our next twenty years together."

When both partners reach readiness to look forward, this moment marks the beginning of the most rewarding phase of marriage renaissance: creating a compelling shared vision that pulls you toward a purposeful future together.

Vision Architecture Process

Creating your shared vision involves five key steps:

1. **Independent dreaming** - Separately identify your hopes and aspirations.
2. **Vision sharing** - Exchange ideas without judgment or evaluation.
3. **Alignment mapping** - Identify where your visions naturally connect.
4. **Difference honouring** - Acknowledge areas where your visions diverge.
5. **Integration crafting** - Create a shared vision that honours both perspectives.

This process isn't about compromise but creative integration. When Sarah dreamed of meaningful community involvement and Michael envisioned international travel, their integrated vision became volunteering with a global literacy organisation, combining service with adventure in a way neither had initially imagined.

"I would never have thought of this on my own," Michael said as they researched teaching opportunities in Guatemala. "This is better than what either of us pictured separately."

Permission statement: "We give ourselves permission to dream boldly about our shared future, creating a vision as meaningful and purposeful as our parenting years."

Vision Implementation Framework

A vision without action remains a fantasy. Sarah and Michael implemented their shared vision through this framework:

1. **Three-year horizon** - What do you want your relationship to embody in three years?
2. **One-year milestones** - What specific achievements will mark progress this year?
3. **Quarterly projects** - What concrete initiatives will you undertake each quarter?
4. **Monthly practices** - What regular activities will build toward your vision?
5. **Weekly commitments** - What specific actions will you take each week?

This cascading structure connected their grand vision to daily actions, making transformation manageable. Their three-year vision of becoming "global literacy ambassadors" translated to a one-year milestone of completing an ESL teaching certification, quarterly projects of language study, monthly volunteer sessions at their local literacy centre, and weekly Spanish practice together.

"Having these concrete steps makes our big dream feel possible," Sarah noted as they added the framework to their shared calendar.

Permission statement: "We give ourselves permission to structure our time around our shared vision, recognising that our relationship deserves the same planning we once gave to our children's development."

Applying Your Permission Framework to Your Marriage
One year into their empty nest, Sarah noticed something meaningful during their weekly planning breakfast.

"I'm still scheduling everything around your preferences," she told Michael. "That's a pattern we established when your work schedule was less flexible during the parenting years, but it doesn't make sense anymore."

This insight highlights how the permission framework you've developed throughout this book applies specifically to your marriage renaissance. Like Sarah, you may discover deeply ingrained relationship patterns that no longer serve you—patterns that require conscious permission to change.

Apply the GRANT framework specifically to your marriage:

1. **Ground** - Acknowledge the foundation of your relationship and validate your parenting journey together.
2. **Reclaim** - Identify small relationship permissions you can practice daily.
3. **Amplify** - Expand permission to redesign significant aspects of your relationship.
4. **Normalise** - Create relationship permission triggers and rituals.
5. **Transcend** - Develop a relationship entitlement mindset for your partnership.

When Sarah applied this framework, she moved from resentment about scheduling inequity to a constructive conversation with Michael about creating more balanced decision-making. This small but significant shift represented their evolving relationship dynamics.

"I never realised how many of our parenting roles shaped our patterns," Michael reflected. "It's like we're learning to be a couple all over again, but with decades of shared history."

Permission statement: "We give ourselves permission to redesign our relationship with the same creativity and care that we're bringing to our transformations."

The empty nest transition offers what few marriages receive—a natural opportunity to consciously recreate your relationship. By applying your architect mindset to your partnership, you transform what could be a period of awkward rediscovery into the foundation for the most fulfilling phase of your relationship.

Nine months after their awkward breakfast table silence, Sarah and Michael celebrated their wedding anniversary with a sunset hike to where they'd gotten engaged twenty-six years earlier.

"I never expected this empty nest to bring us closer," Sarah admitted as they toasted with champagne. "But in some ways, I feel like we're getting to know each other all over again—and I like who we're becoming together."

In the next chapter, we'll explore how to extend your architectural capabilities beyond your immediate family to create meaningful community connections that provide purpose, contribution, and legacy.

Chapter 19

COMMUNITY CONTRIBUTION DESIGN

THE most powerful gifts come from those who know their limits.

Claire stood at the entrance of the Wellington Community Centre, her heart racing with a familiar mix of excitement and anxiety. Just four months after her youngest had left for university, she was taking her first steps back into community involvement. The volunteer coordinator had already mentioned three different programs that needed help. As Claire nodded automatically, she felt the old pattern emerging—the instinct to say yes to everything, to lose herself in others' needs. Then she remembered her permission journal entry from that morning: "I give myself permission to contribute without self-sacrifice." She took a deep breath and spoke words that would have been impossible six months earlier: "I'd like to focus on just the literacy program for now, and see how that fits my schedule."

Your journey through the empty nest transition has brought you to a critical crossroads. Having reclaimed your permission foundation and expanded it across various life domains, you now face the challenge that derails many empty nesters: creating meaningful community connections without reverting to the self-sacrifice patterns of your parenting years. This chapter will guide you through designing contribution systems honouring your wisdom and entitled freedom.

Phase One: Identifying Your Wisdom Currency
Ellen hunched over her kitchen table, surrounded by brochures from local charities. "I should be doing something useful," she muttered, "but nothing feels right." After twenty-three years of parenting and fifteen years caring for ageing

parents, Ellen faced what she called "the double empty"—both children and caregiving responsibilities vanishing within months. During our coaching session, she expressed her frustration: "I have all this knowledge about navigating healthcare for elderly parents, supporting teenagers through college applications, managing family crises—but nowhere to share it. It feels like I'm holding valuable currency I can't spend."

Ellen's dilemma illustrates the wisdom-sharing paradox that affects many empty nesters. You've accumulated invaluable expertise through decades of life experience, but finding the right contexts to share it presents complex challenges:

1. **The Relevance Gap**: Your wisdom isn't universally valuable—it has specific applications where it shines and others where it may be unwelcome.

2. **The Boundary Dilemma**: How do you offer insights without overstepping or appearing judgmental?

3. **The Platform Problem**: Where can you share your expertise in formats others can receive?

Start by creating your Wisdom Inventory—a critical first step that most empty nesters skip, rushing to fill their calendars with random volunteer work. This structured assessment will map your expertise against potential contribution contexts.

Expertise Domain	Experience Level	Potential Value	Appropriate Sharing Contexts
College application guidance	Expert (guided three children)	High	Parent workshops, school programs, and first-generation college student mentoring
Family financial management	Intermediate (20 years)	Moderate	Women's financial literacy programs, single-parent support groups
Healthcare navigation	Expert (managed parents' care)	Very high	Hospital volunteer programs, caregiver support organisations
Work/life balance strategies	Developing (still learning)	Moderate	Peer support groups, mutual learning environments

After completing this assessment, Ellen had a revelation. While her eldercare knowledge wasn't currently relevant to her adult children, it was desperately needed by families navigating the system. She approached a local hospital's patient advocacy program, where her expertise directly benefited families facing similar challenges to those she'd overcome. Within weeks, she found herself engaged in work that valued her specific wisdom while respecting her time boundaries.

Your wisdom doesn't belong everywhere. The first step toward meaningful contribution is matching your expertise with contexts where it's actively sought and appreciated. This isn't selfishness—strategic generosity ensures your offerings land where they create genuine impact.

Phase Two: Architecting Contribution Projects with Value Alignment
Hannah couldn't sleep after watching a documentary about environmental destruction. With her children launched, she felt a new responsibility toward future generations—a sense that her contribution should extend beyond her family. The next morning, she joined three environmental organisations, signed up for weekly beach cleanups, and volunteered to coordinate a fundraiser. Two months later, she sat in my office, exhausted, ready to abandon everything.

"I care deeply about this cause," she explained, "but I'm right back in the same pattern—overcommitted, overwhelmed, and unable to enjoy any of it."

Hannah's experience reveals a common empty nester trap: the all-or-nothing contribution approach. Without the ready-made parenting structure to define your giving, it's easy to either overcommit or completely disengage. The solution isn't reducing your contribution—it's architecting it with the same care you'd give any critical project.

Follow this four-step process to design contribution projects aligned with your values:

Step 1: Value Clarification. Ask yourself these essential questions:

- What causes or communities consistently capture my attention?
- Which social issues align with my core values?
- What legacy do I want to create beyond my family impact?

Step 2: Contribution Method Assessment. Identify your natural contribution style:

- Direct service (hands-on involvement)
- Knowledge sharing (teaching, mentoring)
- Resource provision (fundraising, material support)
- Leadership (organising, directing initiatives)
- Creative contribution (artistic or innovative solutions)

Step 3: Energy Evaluation. Assess potential contributions against these criteria:

- Does this type of involvement energise or drain me?
- Does it utilise my natural strengths or require constant strain?
- Does it provide the connection and meaning I'm seeking?

Step 4: Boundary Definition. Create clear parameters:

- Specific time commitments (hours per week/month)
- Defined role boundaries
- Clear start and end dates
- Regular reassessment points

Following this process, Hannah realised that while environmental protection genuinely mattered to her, she needed project-based rather than ongoing commitments. She also discovered that her organisational skills were more valuable than her physical presence at clean-ups. This led her to design a quarterly fundraising event for her favourite environmental organisation—a contribution honouring her values and her need for time flexibility.

To maintain these boundaries, adopt the Project Prospectus approach. Before committing to any community involvement, complete this template:

Project Element	Questions to Answer	Example Responses
Purpose	Why does this matter to me?	"I value education access and want to help first-generation college students."
Contribution	What specific value will I add?	"I'll mentor two students through their application process, sharing my experience guiding my children."

Time Frame	When will this begin and end?	"September through January, concluding when applications are submitted."
Time Commitment	How many hours weekly/monthly?	"Two hours weekly, scheduled on Tuesday afternoons."
Energy Assessment	Does this energise or drain me?	"One-on-one mentoring energises me, while large group presentations drain me."
Exit Strategy	How will I conclude or transition this commitment?	"After applications are submitted, I'll provide two follow-up sessions, then transition to the next mentor cycle."

This structured approach prevents the endless, undefined commitments that gradually erode your entitled freedom. By architecting your contribution with clear boundaries, you ensure it enhances rather than diminishes your next chapter.

Phase Three: Building Intergenerational Connections Beyond Family
Robert refreshed his phone for the fourth time that hour, then set it down with a sigh. His daughter hadn't responded to his good morning text, and his son's weekly call wasn't scheduled until Sunday. "Is this what the next twenty years look like?" he wondered aloud to his empty living room. "Waiting for my children to have time for me?" The thought left him feeling hollow and irrelevant.

Many empty nesters make a critical mistake: they limit their intergenerational connections exclusively to family relationships. While maintaining bonds with adult children is essential, restricting your interaction with younger generations to family roles creates vulnerability and missed opportunities for growth.

Intergenerational connections outside family contexts offer unique benefits that family relationships often can't provide:

- **Expectation-free interactions** unburdened by family history or dynamics.
- **Fresh perspectives** that challenge your thinking in ways adult children may not.
- **Technological fluency** gained through natural knowledge exchange.
- **Mentoring opportunities** that utilise your wisdom without parental complications.

- **Identity reinforcement** beyond your family roles.

Margaret, a retired accounting professor, initially worried she'd lose connection with younger generations after her twins left home. Rather than focusing exclusively on her new role as a grandmother, she joined a community theatre group with members ranging from 16 to 82.

"The relationships are completely different from family connections," she explained during our group coaching session. "There's no history, no expectations —just shared interest in theatre. I've formed genuine friendships with people three and four decades younger than me who would never be interested in my life advice, but we exchange perspectives naturally through our shared creative work. Last week, a 23-year-old cast member asked for my guidance on her career path. The conversation happened organically, without the resistance that often comes when I try to advise my children."

To architect intergenerational connections in your community, implement these specific strategies:

1. **Join mixed-age interest groups** focused on activities you genuinely enjoy: community choirs, theatre groups, hiking clubs, or art classes naturally attract diverse age ranges.
2. **Explore formal mentoring programs** in areas aligned with your expertise: Many colleges, schools, and community organisations have structured programs that match experienced adults with younger mentees.
3. **Participate in skill exchanges** where you teach expertise from your background while learning new skills from younger participants: cooking classes, digital literacy programs, or craft workshops often facilitate this mutual learning.
4. **Engage in civic improvement projects** that attract diverse participants: community gardens, neighbourhood revitalisation efforts, or local advocacy groups typically draw people across generations.
5. **Consider co-learning environments** where hierarchy is minimised: workshops, classes, or creative ventures where everyone is simultaneously student and contributor create natural connections.

These relationships satisfy your need for significance and connection without imposing expectations on family interactions. They also provide a crucial element of your empty nest transformation—identity expansion beyond the parent role that defined you for decades.

Phase Four: Creating Permission-Based Boundaries for Sustainable Giving
Teresa left the community centre orientation feeling simultaneously excited and uneasy. She'd intended to volunteer just two hours weekly at the food bank. Still, she somehow left having agreed to chair the fundraising committee—a position the previous volunteer had described as "practically a full-time job." Driving home, Teresa recognised the familiar sensation in her stomach. "I've done it again," she thought. "Twenty years of putting everyone else first, and I still can't say no."

The boundary-setting challenge represents the most crucial aspect of community contribution design. After decades of placing others' needs before your own, maintaining healthy boundaries requires vigilance and structured systems. Your permission work in previous chapters provides the foundation, but specific boundary-enforcement mechanisms are necessary when engaging with community organisations.

Teresa's experience illustrates a familiar pattern—the immediate slide back into overcommitment when facing appreciation and need. She had spent weeks developing her permission practices at home, but collapsed in the face of the volunteer coordinator's enthusiasm. To prevent this boundary erosion, implement these four protective structures:

1. Permission Priming
Before entering any potential contribution situation, practice your permission statement. Teresa developed this ritual: before entering any volunteer setting, she would sit in her car and write in her permission journal, "I give myself permission to contribute in ways that honour my boundaries and priorities." This simple practice activates your permission foundation when you need it most.

2. The Pause Protocol
Even after months of practice, many empty nesters find it challenging to decline requests in the moment. Develop and memorise this standard response: "This sounds like important work. I need to check my current commitments before I can give you a thoughtful answer. I'll get back to you by [specific time]." This creates space for boundary assessment away from social pressure.

3. The Contribution Contract

For any significant commitment, create an explicit written agreement that outlines:

- Specific responsibilities
- Time limitations
- Renewal decision points
- Conditions for stepping back

After her initial overcommitment, Teresa implemented this system. She met with the director and renegotiated her role, agreeing to mentor a younger volunteer in grant writing rather than chairing the entire committee. They documented the arrangement, including three months with a specific reassessment date. This structured agreement allowed Teresa to contribute meaningfully while maintaining her established boundaries.

4. The Weekly Contribution Audit

Every Sunday evening, spend five minutes reviewing your community commitments against these questions:

- Does this contribution still align with my values and priorities?
- Is the energy exchange positive or negative?
- Am I maintaining my entitled boundaries?
- What adjustments would make this more sustainable?

This regular assessment prevents the slow boundary erosion that often happens over time, allowing you to adjust before reaching burnout.

These systems aren't about limiting your giving—they're about transforming how you give. Your community contribution should come from your entitled self-direction rather than habitual self-sacrifice. This shift doesn't reduce your impact; it makes it sustainable and authentic.

As Marion, a participant in our empty nest group, observed after six months of practising these strategies: "I'm contributing more meaningfully now that I've learned to say no. I genuinely want to be there when I say yes, not because

I feel obligated. People can feel the difference—I'm bringing my whole self to fewer commitments than my depleted self to too many."

As you architect your community contribution design, remember that the most meaningful giving comes from freedom rather than obligation. The entitled contribution you create now will form a significant part of your empty nest identity—one that honours both your wisdom and your right to self-determination.

In the next chapter, we'll explore how to architect digital relationships with adult children, creating technological boundaries that maintain meaningful connections while respecting independence in our constantly connected world.

Chapter 20

Digital Relationship Architecture

Susan flinched as her phone lit up with a notification, then exhaled when she saw her son's name on the screen after hours of anxious waiting.

The brief text message—"Mom, I'm fine. Just busy with work. Talk later."—brought a conflicting wave of relief and disappointment. David had moved across the country six months ago, and though technology promised to keep them connected, their digital relationship felt more strained than their in-person one ever had. Was she reaching out too much? Not enough? The three texts she'd sent today suddenly seemed excessive, but the maternal instinct to check on him hadn't diminished just because he'd moved out. Susan set her phone down on the kitchen counter and wondered, not for the first time, how something designed to connect people could make her feel so isolated.

"I never thought I'd need a strategy for texting my son," she confided during our empty nest workshop the following week. "But I'm realising that's exactly what I need—a plan for how we stay connected without me feeling like I'm intruding or him feeling like he's being monitored."

Susan's experience echoes what countless empty nesters face today—a challenge no previous generation of parents navigated. While your parents or grandparents might have settled for weekly phone calls or handwritten letters after their children left home, you now inhabit a world of instant communication possibilities that create opportunities and unexpected complications. This chapter will guide you through creating a thoughtful architecture for your digital relationships, transforming potential sources of anxiety into bridges that strengthen your connection while respecting everyone's independence.

Creating Healthy Technology Boundaries with Adult Children
"It felt like rejection every time she didn't pick up," Janice admitted, describing her first months after her daughter Emma moved out. The pain in her voice was palpable as she shared her story with our empty nest support group. "I'd call multiple times a day because that's what we did when she lived at home—we talked constantly. But now it seemed like she was avoiding me."

Janice's breakthrough came after a boundary-setting conversation where Emma explained that phone calls disrupted her workday concentration. "She wasn't rejecting me—just working differently than I understood," Janice explained. "Once I realised that, we could find a solution."

They agreed on scheduled, twice-weekly calls and used texts for quick updates, transforming their communication pattern from a source of tension to a connection they both enjoyed. "Now, when we talk, the conversations are so much better because we're both fully present instead of one of us feeling interrupted," Janice shared, her relief evident.

Generational differences in technology use create the first hurdle in digital relationship architecture. While you might value a lengthy phone call, your adult child may prefer brief text exchanges or social media interactions. Neither approach is inherently superior—they reflect different lived experiences with technology. Your challenge is to bridge this gap with thoughtful boundaries that work for everyone involved.

Digital Boundary Framework
Begin your digital boundary construction with these four foundational principles:

1. **Communication Preferences Assessment**: Have an honest conversation about preferred communication methods, timing, and frequency. Instead of assuming your adult child shares your preferences, ask direct questions: "What's the best way to reach you for non-urgent matters?" and "Are there certain times when you prefer not to receive calls or texts?"

2. **Response Expectation Setting**: Establish mutual understanding about response times. When Maria implemented this with her son Carlos, she was surprised by his answer: "He wanted me to mark texts that needed a quick response with a specific emoji. He would answer the rest when he had downtime. This simple system prevented so much misunderstanding."

3. **Privacy Respect Parameters**: Recognise that your adult child's social media presence isn't primarily meant for parental surveillance. Respect their digital space by asking before commenting on or sharing their posts. Michael learned this lesson after his daughter Hannah asked him to stop commenting on her professional LinkedIn posts: "I thought I was being supportive, but she explained that her LinkedIn was for professional networking, and my dad's comments, while well-meaning, didn't fit the context."

4. **Regular Boundary Reassessment**: Communication needs evolve. Schedule occasional check-ins to see whether your digital interaction patterns are working for both of you. Ellen and her daughter now have a quick "communication check-in" during their monthly dinner: "Just a simple 'How are our calls and texts working for you lately?' opens the door to adjustments before frustrations build."

This framework transforms vague worries about "bothering" your child into clear agreements that reduce anxiety for everyone involved. The most important element is approaching the conversation with genuine curiosity rather than defensive justification of your preferences.

Balancing Connection with Independence in Digital Spaces

Margaret couldn't sleep after seeing her son's Instagram post from a beach party. Her mind raced with worries about sunburn, alcohol, and water safety. By morning, she'd sent three concerned texts, none of which he'd answered.

"When he finally responded twelve hours later, he was frustrated that I was 'monitoring' him," Margaret shared during our coaching session. "He said it made him not want to post anything because he felt he was still being parented from afar."

Margaret's experience highlights one of the most challenging aspects of digital relationships: the constant visibility into your adult child's life through social media creates both opportunities and complications. While it provides reassurance and connection points, it can also trigger anxiety and overreaction to everyday young adult experiences.

The key to navigating this challenge is developing an "entitled response approach" to digital information: you're entitled to feel concerned when you see something worrying, but not entitled to demand immediate reassurance or express every concern that crosses your mind.

Digital Independence Matrix

Use this matrix to guide your responses to information you encounter in digital spaces:

Information Type	Entitled Response	Boundary Overstepping
Social Posts	Enjoy seeing their activities without commenting on everything	Questioning choices, expressing worry, and critiquing friends
Life Updates	Express genuine interest and support	Offering unsolicited advice or expecting immediate responses
Absence of Posts	Assume they're busy living their lives	Sending multiple "Are you ok?" messages or assuming something's wrong
Concerning Content	Express care privately with "I noticed X and wanted to check in"	Public comments about Behaviour or demanding explanations

Sarah applied this matrix when her daughter posted about a job interview disappointment: "My instinct was to call immediately with advice and reassurance—that's what I would have done when she lived at home. Instead, I paused and sent a simple text: 'I saw your post. That company missed out on someone amazing. I'm here if you want to talk.'"

The result surprised her: "She called me later that evening on her terms, and we had a much deeper conversation than if I'd pushed. She was ready to talk when she reached out, not defensive because I'd demanded her attention."

By distinguishing between entitled responses and boundary overstepping, you create space for authentic connection that respects independence. This approach transforms social media from a source of anxiety to a window that provides appropriate insight into your adult child's world.

Using Technology to Support Rather Than Replace Relationships

Robert's weekly Zoom calls with his daughter Amelia had become increasingly short and perfunctory. "We'd ask the standard questions—how's work, how's the apartment, any plans this weekend—and be done in fifteen minutes. It felt like we were both checking a box rather than connecting," he shared.

The turning point came when Robert realised they needed a purpose beyond the call. "I suggested we try cooking the same recipe simultaneously while on video chat. The first time was a disaster—we were covered in flour and laughing so hard we could barely finish the recipe. But it was the most fun we'd had together in months."

This simple shift transformed their digital interaction from obligation to a meaningful shared experience. Now they alternate between cooking together, watching the same movie and texting reactions, or even taking virtual museum tours simultaneously.

Robert's discovery illustrates a crucial principle: digital communication works best by enhancing real-world connections rather than substituting for them. Text messages, video calls, and social media interactions can enrich your relationship, but they can't fully replace the quality of in-person time together.

Digital Connection Enhancement Strategies

Transform your digital communication with these approaches:

1. **Shared Digital Experiences**: Create moments of connection despite physical distance through shared activities. Linda and her son downloaded a chess app and now maintain an ongoing game: "Sometimes we make just one move a day, but it's a touchpoint that keeps us connected without pressure."

2. **Purposeful Communication**: Send specific, thoughtful messages rather than generic check-ins. "I saw this article about sustainable architecture and thought of your senior project", shows you're paying attention to what matters to them. Thomas sends his daughter links to news about her favourite bands: "It gives us something specific to talk about beyond the usual updates."

3. **Digital Care Packages**: Use technology to arrange real-world surprises that show you're thinking of them. When Jessica's son mentioned he was swamped with finals, she placed a food delivery to his apartment: "It was a way to 'take care of him' that was appropriate for his age and independence level."

4. **Photo Exchanges**: Share images that wouldn't make it to social media—the everyday moments that build connection. Diane and her daughter have a dedicated text thread just for photos of their dogs: "It's lighthearted and consistent, keeping us connected when we don't have time for deeper conversations."

5. **Voice and Video Priority**: For meaningful conversations, opt for richer communication channels that capture tone, facial expressions, and emotional nuances. Paul realised text messages were creating misunderstandings with his son: "Now we have a rule that anything emotional gets upgraded to a call. It's prevented so many unnecessary tensions."

These strategies create meaningful connections without creating burdensome expectations for constant communication. The goal isn't maximising communication quantity but optimising its quality and purpose.

Developing Digital Rituals That Enhance Rather Than Detract

Jennifer stared at her phone every Sunday morning, waiting for her week's highlight—her son's "Sunday snapshot." After moving abroad for work, they had established a simple ritual of exchanging one photo each week that captured something meaningful from their lives.

"Sometimes it's just a sunset or a meal, other times it's something more significant, like a new friend or a work achievement," Jennifer explained. "But that single photo exchange often leads to deeper conversations about what's happening in our lives. It's a small touchpoint that keeps us connected without being intrusive."

What makes Jennifer's ritual successful is that it adds value for both her and her son without creating a burden. It's appropriately sized, flexible enough to accommodate occasional misses when life gets busy and has naturally evolved.

Digital rituals—regular, meaningful technology-based interactions—provide structure and connection without becoming obligations. The key is creating rituals that enhance rather than complicate your relationship.

Digital Ritual Design Framework

Design sustainable digital rituals using these guidelines:

1. **Mutually Beneficial**: The ritual should add value for both of you, not just satisfy your need for connection. When David established a weekend video call with his son, it kept getting postponed until he realised the timing conflicted with his son's social life. They switched to Tuesday evenings and found both were more consistently available and engaged.

2. **Appropriately Sized**: Start with small, manageable rituals that can evolve rather than ambitious plans that become burdensome. Katherine initially proposed a daily check-in call with her daughter, but quickly realised it was unsustainable. Their modified approach—a quick voice memo exchange three times a week—provided a connection without overwhelming either of their schedules.

3. **Flexibility Built-In**: Create room for occasional misses without guilt when life gets busy. The Roberts family established a monthly virtual game night but included an automatic one-week postponement option if needed: "Having that flexibility built in from the start meant we didn't feel like failures when scheduling conflicts arose."

4. **Evolution Expected**: Recognise that effective rituals will change as your relationship evolves and circumstances shift. When Mia's daughter started graduate school, their morning text exchange no longer worked with her new schedule. Instead of abandoning the ritual, they moved to an evening gratitude exchange that better suited her changed routine.

Successful digital rituals might include:

- Monthly family video calls with a loose theme or activity.
- Weekly article or podcast exchanges related to shared interests.
- Photo challenges around seasonal themes.
- Digital celebration traditions for milestones.

Lisa created a joint digital photo album with her two adult children: "We all upload photos to a shared album called 'Notice This'. It's our way of sharing small moments that might not warrant a text or call but keep us connected to each other's daily lives. It's become a cherished timeline of our family's ongoing story, even as we live separately."

The most successful digital rituals often start small and gain significance through consistency rather than beginning with grand expectations.

Permission in Practice: Digital Relationship Entitlement

Patricia stared at her phone, composing and deleting the same text message three times. She wanted to share an article she thought her daughter would enjoy, but found herself paralysed by questions: Was she texting too much? Would her daughter find it annoying? Was she overstepping?

This pattern repeated several times a week until Patricia applied her permission framework to digital communication. During a permission journal session, she wrote: "I permit myself to text my daughter about things I find interesting without worrying if I'm bothering her. I also permit myself not to expect an immediate response."

This simple shift transformed her digital communication. "Now I share things because I genuinely want to, not because I'm seeking reassurance about our relationship," Patricia explained. "Ironically, our text exchanges have become more natural and enjoyable because they come from a place of sharing rather than anxiety."

Applying your permission framework to digital relationships means recognising your entitlement to:

- Initiate meaningful communication without guilt or anxiety.
- Allow messages to go unanswered for appropriate periods.
- Maintain your digital boundaries around availability.
- Express genuine concern when warranted.
- Enjoy a digital connection without expectations that it replicates in-person relationships.

Andrew described his entitlement breakthrough: "I realised I had been treating every unanswered text as rejection rather than giving my son the space to respond when convenient. Now I send messages expecting they're received with love, even if they're not answered immediately, or sometimes at all. This perspective has removed so much unnecessary pain from our digital relationship."

This entitled approach to digital communication creates the foundation for an authentic connection that evolves naturally as you and your adult children grow and change.

As you develop your skills as a digital relationship architect, you're building capabilities that extend beyond technology. These same principles of boundary-setting, expectation management, and entitled communication will serve you well when facing unexpected challenges in your empty nest journey. In the next chapter, we'll explore how to maintain your transition architect identity during unanticipated developments, using your permission framework as a resilience tool for whatever the future might bring.

Chapter 21

NAVIGATING UNEXPECTED TRANSITIONS

REBECCA stared at the suitcases in her hallway with love and dread. Three months earlier, she had transformed her daughter's bedroom into a writing sanctuary with a vintage desk, floor-to-ceiling bookshelves, and a reading chair positioned perfectly by the window. Each morning, she had settled into this space with a cup of tea, working on the novel she'd postponed for twenty years. But now, Megan was coming home—her post-graduation job opportunity had fallen through, and she needed a place to regroup for "just a few months." As Rebecca folded the colourful quilt she'd draped over her reading chair, she felt a familiar sensation in her chest: the quiet surrender of her needs, the automatic shift back into mom-mode. She wondered if these past months of transformation had been merely a temporary fantasy.

The empty nest path rarely unfolds as neatly as we imagine. As you begin settling into your new routines and identity, unexpected challenges emerge—adult children return home, health issues arise, or ageing parents need support. These disruptions can feel like they're invalidating all your progress. You might wonder if your permission to prioritise yourself was premature or if your architect identity was merely a temporary illusion. This chapter addresses the reality that transitions are rarely linear and provides tools to maintain your progress when life takes unexpected turns.

Applying Your Architect Mindset to Unanticipated Challenges

"I guess the universe thought I was getting too comfortable with my freedom," Barbara laughed, though her eyes didn't join in.

The morning her daughter Sophie called from university, voice breaking with anxiety and the confession that she couldn't handle the pressure anymore, Barbara felt her stomach drop. Within hours, she had transformed into crisis-management mom—making lists, researching therapists, and clearing out her art supplies from what had been Sophie's bedroom before becoming Barbara's studio six months earlier.

"I dismantled my studio in record time," she told me during our coaching session, her fingers nervously twisting the silver bracelet she wore. "Eight months of building this new life took me less than a day to erase. I cancelled my book club membership, postponed the weekend art retreat I'd finally allowed myself to book, and told my painting group I wouldn't return for a while."

Barbara paused, looking down at her hands. "The worst part wasn't even the physical act of taking down my easel or boxing up my supplies. It was the voice in my head saying, 'See? You were playing pretend. This is who you are—just mom, nothing more.'"

Barbara initially missed that Sophie's return didn't invalidate her architect identity—it was being called upon for its most significant test. The question wasn't whether to support her daughter; it was how to help her while maintaining core elements of her newly established self.

Two weeks after Sophie's return, I visited Barbara's home. She greeted me with visible exhaustion but led me to the sunroom at the back of the house. To my surprise, her easel and a small table with organised painting supplies stood there.

"It's not my full studio," she admitted, "but I realised something important. If I completely abandoned my painting—the thing that reconnects me to myself—I wouldn't be helping Sophie. I'd just be modelling the same pattern of anxiety and self-sacrifice that she's struggling with herself."

Barbara had made a crucial discovery: her architect mindset wasn't a luxury for ideal circumstances but an essential tool during a crisis. The skills she'd developed through the GRANT system were precisely what she needed to navigate this unexpected challenge.

"The turning point came when I stopped asking if I should help Sophie or care for myself," Barbara explained, mixing colours on her palette as we talked. "Instead, I asked myself: How would an architect design a solution that addresses both needs?"

Your architect mindset becomes most powerful during these unexpected transitions. The skills you've developed aren't indulgences to be abandoned when challenges arise—they're precisely the tools you need to navigate complex situations with wisdom:

- **Differentiate between adaptations and regressions**: Barbara modified her art space without completely abandoning her creative practice.
- **Apply selective flexibility**: She maintained her Monday morning painting sessions while adjusting other aspects of her schedule to support Sophie.
- **Identify permission patterns**: Feeling guilty about maintaining boundaries, she recognised her automatic self-sacrifice response.
- **Reframe challenges as design problems**: Rather than seeing Sophie's return as a failure, she viewed it as a new situation to architect thoughtfully.

This mindset shift transforms everything. Instead of seeing challenges as evidence that you weren't entitled to self-prioritisation, you recognise them as situations demanding your most skilled identity work.

Creating Permission Frameworks for Crisis Response

The call came at 2:17 AM on a Tuesday. Thomas fumbled for his phone in the darkness, his heart racing before hearing the news.

"Dad's fallen," his sister's voice trembled through the speaker. "They're taking him to Memorial Hospital. Can you meet me there?"

Thomas had prepared for many scenarios during his thirty-year teaching career—classroom emergencies, student crises, even the occasional school lockdown. But nothing had prepared him for the sudden shift from newly retired empty-nester to primary caregiver for his 83-year-old father.

The first week after his father's fall passed in a blur of hospital corridors, doctor consultations, and hurried meals from vending machines. By week two, as they settled into a rehabilitation facility routine, Thomas noticed the toll it was taking. His sleep deteriorated. He'd abandoned his morning meditation practice—the cornerstone of his mental health since his divorce a decade earlier. His twice-weekly swim sessions, once non-negotiable fixtures in his calendar, were forgotten as days blurred in the beige-walled rehab facility.

"I'll sleep when this is over," he told himself, ignoring the irony that "over" had no clear endpoint with his father's condition.

It wasn't until he found himself snapping at a well-meaning nurse that Thomas recognised what was happening. He was falling into the same trap that had claimed so many empty nesters during crises: permission regression.

Crises demand response systems, not permission abandonment.

When genuine emergencies arise, the automatic response for most empty nesters is to abandon all permission structures. This approach fails both you and those you're supporting. A more effective strategy is to develop permission protocols designed explicitly for crisis periods.

Permission Crisis Protocol

Crisis Level	Self-Care Minimum	Response Guidelines	Permission Language
Level 1: Minor disruption (unexpected visits, temporary help needed)	Maintain 80% of regular routines	Adjust timing, but not the elimination of core activities	"I'll help with [specific task] after completing my morning routine."
Level 2: Moderate challenge (extended stay, ongoing support needs)	Maintain 60% of routines, prioritising essentials	Negotiate clear boundaries around specific times/spaces	"I'll set aside Tuesday and Thursday afternoons to help, while preserving my morning writing time."
Level 3: Significant crisis (health emergency, major life disruption)	Identify and protect 30-40% non-negotiable self-care	Create explicit temporary arrangements with defined endpoints	"During this three-week recovery period, I'll help with daily care but will continue my evening walks and maintain my therapy appointment."

That evening, Thomas sat down with his notepad and created his crisis protocol. He identified his non-negotiables—his morning meditation and twice-weekly swim—and designed a plan around them. The next morning, he called a family meeting with his siblings.

"I can handle Dad's morning medication and breakfast five days a week," he explained, surprising himself with the steadiness in his voice, "but I need to maintain my 7:00-8:00 AM meditation practice, and I'll need coverage on Tuesdays and Thursdays for my swimming sessions. Those aren't optional for my mental health."

The silence that followed felt eternal. Thomas braced himself for resistance, for accusations of selfishness. Instead, his sister Diane nodded.

"That makes sense," she said. "I can cover Tuesdays before work. And this helps me know exactly when you need support instead of trying to guess."

By maintaining these core elements, Thomas provided better support than if he'd sacrificed everything and become depleted. His permission framework enhanced his caregiving capacity.

Three months later, Thomas's father had recovered enough to return home with part-time care. During our coaching session, Thomas reflected on what he'd learned.

"Before we did all this permission work, I would have approached Dad's fall completely differently," he admitted. "I would have dropped everything—and then resented it, burned out, and probably been a terrible caregiver as a result."

He pulled out a worn index card from his wallet. On it, I could see his handwritten crisis protocol—five simple points he'd reviewed daily during the most challenging weeks.

"I never would have thought something as simple as maintaining my morning meditation could make such a difference," he said. "But those quiet moments each morning kept me grounded when everything else felt chaotic. And having clear boundaries made it easier for everyone involved—there was no guesswork about when I was available."

When creating your crisis protocol, focus on these key practices:

1. **Pre-authorise essential self-care**: Before crisis strikes, identify the minimum self-care activities you'll protect at all costs—whether a daily walk, therapy appointments, or specific sleep requirements.

2. **Establish time boundaries**: Replace open-ended availability with specific timeframes for assistance—"I can help between 2:00-5:00 PM" instead of "Call me anytime".

3. **Implement permission pauses**: Train yourself to take 60-second breaks before responding to requests, creating space to consider whether your automatic "yes" serves everyone best.

4. **Use permission forwarding**: Explicitly schedule future self-care for intense caregiving periods—"After these two weeks of helping Dad, I'm taking a full day at the spa".

5. **Maintain permission language**: Continue using explicit self-authorisation vocabulary even during crises—"I give myself permission to take thirty minutes for lunch while Dad naps".

This framework prevents the typical pattern where a temporary crisis permanently erases permission progress. By maintaining even minimal permission practices during challenging times, you preserve the foundation of your entitled identity.

Maintaining Entitlement During Boomerang Situations

Jennifer hesitated before opening her son's bedroom door, feeling like an intruder in what was now her meditation space.

Ryan had been gone for almost a year—enough time for Jennifer to convert his bedroom into a tranquil sanctuary with soft lighting, cushions for meditation, and carefully selected plants. As she surveyed the space central to her new identity, she felt a knot in her stomach. Ryan had called that morning. He'd lost his job and needed to return home "until he found something new."

"Of course you can come home," she'd said automatically, mentally dismantling her sanctuary to make room for his return.

The "boomerang" phenomenon—adult children temporarily returning to the family home—has become increasingly common. Economic pressures, relationship changes, health challenges, or career transitions often bring young adults back to their parents' homes for weeks to years.

Three weeks after Ryan's return, I met Jennifer for coffee. Dark circles shadowed her eyes, and she clutched her mug like a lifeline.

"It happened so fast," she admitted, her voice barely above a whisper. "Within days, I was cooking his favourite meals every night, doing his laundry with the special detergent he likes, and rearranging my book club schedule because he wanted me home to discuss his job applications. Suddenly, I was a full-time mom again, as if the past year hadn't happened."

Jennifer described how she'd dismantled her meditation space entirely, returned the furniture to storage, and moved her cushions to a corner of her bedroom where they now sat unused.

"What bothers me most is how automatic it was," she said. "I didn't even consider alternatives. It was like all my permission work vanished when he needed me."

The key to maintaining your entitled identity during boomerang periods is establishing a fundamentally different household arrangement than what existed when your child was younger:

During our second session, I shared with Jennifer the framework that had helped dozens of my clients navigate boomerang situations successfully. Together, we drafted an "Adult Household Agreement"—a compassionate but clear document outlining how two adults could share a home while respecting each other's independence.

Adult Household Agreement Sample Elements
1. **Shared responsibility system**: Specific division of household tasks with clear responsibilities.
2. **Space designation**: Explicit boundaries around private spaces and shared areas.
3. **Financial contribution**: Appropriate rent or expense sharing based on the adult child's circumstances.
4. **Time independence**: Clear communication about schedules without accountability requirements.
5. **Support parameters**: Defined boundaries around emotional support and problem-solving.

Jennifer was nervous about presenting these ideas to Ryan. "What if he thinks I don't want him home? What if he takes it as rejection?"

"That's why framing matters," I explained. "This isn't about pushing him away—it's about creating a sustainable arrangement that honours both of you as adults."

The following week, Jennifer arrived at our session with a tentative smile.

"I finally had the conversation with Ryan," she said. "I told him I was thrilled to help during this transition but needed to approach it differently than when he was younger." She paused. "The amazing thing was his response. He seemed relieved. He admitted he'd been worried about falling back into old patterns and losing the independence he'd built over the past year."

Together, they developed a shared Google calendar where they noted their commitments and private time. Ryan took responsibility for specific household tasks, and Jennifer maintained her book club nights and twice-weekly yoga classes. They even found a solution for her meditation practice—Ryan helped her create a smaller but dedicated space in the corner of the home office.

"The strangest part," Jennifer reflected, "is that I think our relationship is stronger now than before he moved back. We're relating as adults, not as parent and child."

For successfully navigating your boomerang situations:

- **Conduct an explicit transition conversation**: Set aside uninterrupted time to discuss how this living arrangement differs from childhood.
- **Create a written agreement**: Document shared expectations to prevent misunderstandings, and review it together to ensure mutual understanding.
- **Establish privacy signals**: Develop clear indicators for when you're unavailable (closed door, headphones on, specific times of day).
- **Maintain key identity practices**: Continue activities central to your post-parenting identity, adjusting logistics without abandoning the practice.
- **Schedule regular reassessments**: Set specific dates to evaluate how the arrangement works, making adjustments as needed.

By approaching boomerang situations as a collaborative design challenge rather than a return to traditional parenting, you protect your entitled identity while supporting your adult child appropriately.

Adapting Your Empty Nest Design to Evolving Circumstances

Helen stared at the two calendar notifications that had appeared within days of each other, feeling as though the universe had a fierce sense of humour.

The first was a confirmation of her mother's cognitive assessment—the official diagnosis of early-stage dementia they'd suspected for months. The second was an unexpected email from her husband Mark's company announcing an early retirement package he couldn't reasonably refuse.

Just six months earlier, Helen had carefully crafted her empty nest design. With both children successfully launched and settled across the country, she had finally established a rhythm that felt right—teaching part-time at the community college, volunteering two afternoons a week at the literacy centre, and dedicating Fridays to her long-postponed watercolour painting. She and Mark had planned their first extended international trip without children—three weeks in Portugal the following spring.

Now, as she sat at her kitchen table surrounded by medical brochures, retirement paperwork, and her carefully constructed schedule that suddenly seemed irrelevant, Helen felt the familiar tightening in her chest—the panic that accompanied disruption.

"It feels like I'm back at square one," she confessed during our next session. "All this work building my identity beyond motherhood, and now I'm facing a new set of caretaking responsibilities. My schedule feels impossible between Mom's appointments and Mark being home all day."

Like many clients, Helen's first instinct was to abandon her design entirely and start from scratch. Instead, I introduced her to the adaptation framework —a systematic approach to modifying rather than discarding her empty nest design as circumstances changed.

Rather than abandoning her plan entirely, she applied a deliberate adaptation process:

1. She assessed which elements of her identity and schedule were essential versus adjustable
2. She identified specific modifications that would accommodate new circumstances
3. She implemented changes incrementally, evaluating the impact at each stage
4. She maintained her core identity throughout the process

Six weeks later, Helen's situation hadn't changed—her mother needed increasing support, and Mark was still adjusting to retirement. But Helen's perspective had transformed entirely.

"What surprised me was discovering that adaptation doesn't mean starting over," Helen reflected as we reviewed her modified schedule. "My entitled identity became more resilient through these changes, not less. I've become more protective of my core needs because I recognise their importance to my wellbeing."

Helen pulled out the adaptation framework worksheet we'd developed together. The simple questions had guided her through what initially felt like an impossible puzzle.

Adaptation Framework Questions

Adaptation Area	Assessment Questions	Design Modifications
Time Structure	Which time blocks are essential vs. flexible? What new requirements must be integrated?	Adjust timing while preserving purpose categories; create bounded periods for new responsibilities.
Purpose Portfolio	Which elements remain viable for this purpose? What new purpose opportunities might emerge?	Modify specific activities while maintaining purpose categories; integrate new circumstances into the purpose framework.
Relationship Patterns	Which relationship boundaries need adjustment? What new communication systems are required?	Update specific protocols while preserving fundamental relationship principles.
Permission Practices	Which permission rituals can be maintained? What new permission needs have emerged?	Adapt permission language to address new challenges; increase permission reinforcement during transitions.

"At first, I thought I'd have to give up my watercolour painting completely," Helen explained. "But working through these questions helped me Realise I could shift my painting from Fridays to Wednesday mornings while Mark played golf. And rather than seeing Mom's appointments as only taking away from my time, I've found ways to integrate some of my purpose elements into our visits—like bringing my sketchbook to capture the gardens at her assisted living facility while she naps."

The adaptation framework helps you maintain continuity of identity while responding to life's inevitable changes. Rather than viewing your empty nest design as a static creation, see it as an evolving blueprint incorporating new information while preserving core principles.

Elizabeth's story further illustrates the power of adaptive architecture. When her husband Robert was diagnosed with a degenerative eye condition requiring numerous specialist appointments and daily therapy, her initial reaction was familiar—complete self-sacrifice.

"I remember calling to cancel my writing workshop registration," Elizabeth told me. "I was in the parking lot outside the ophthalmologist's office, and I assumed I needed to drop everything."

But something stopped her before completing the call. The permission work she'd done over the previous months had taken root deeply enough to create a moment of pause.

"I sat in my car and asked myself: What would an architect do? And I realised an architect wouldn't demolish the entire structure—they would modify the design to incorporate new requirements."

Instead of abandoning her entitled identity, Elizabeth applied her architect mindset to create a modified design that incorporated their new reality:

"I used the adaptation framework to identify which of my activities could shift in timing versus which needed to remain consistent," she explained. "I maintained my morning writing practice and afternoon walk, but adjusted other schedule elements to accommodate Robert's therapy appointments. I even used my waiting time during his longer appointments to work on short writing exercises."

This adaptive approach transformed what could have been a complete regression into an opportunity for strengthening her architectural identity.

Elizabeth shared a surprising discovery during our final session, six months after implementing her adaptation framework.

"The strangest thing has happened," she said, her eyes bright with realisation. "Robert's condition has created limitations, that's true. However, working through this challenge as an architect rather than a caretaker has strengthened my identity. I'm more committed to my writing now than before his diagnosis because I recognise how essential it is to my wellbeing—and therefore to my ability to support him."

She smiled, turning her wedding ring thoughtfully on her finger. "Last week, Robert said something that stopped me in my tracks. He said, 'I'm grateful for your permission work, because the old Elizabeth would have disappeared into taking care of me, and then we'd both suffer.' He's right. By maintaining my identity through this challenge, I'm better equipped to navigate it alongside him."

Your ability to modify your empty nest design while maintaining your core identity is the ultimate test—and evidence—of your transformation. Through this process, you don't just survive unexpected transitions; you architect through them.

Key Takeaway

Rebecca stood in the doorway of what had once been her daughter's bedroom, now a hybrid space. In one corner sat Megan's bed, which she had returned from storage during her unexpected six-month "boomerang" period after her job fell through. But the vintage desk remained by the window, Rebecca's notebook open on its surface, her writing schedule posted above it.

The room told the story of adaptation rather than surrender—of an identity maintained through challenge rather than abandoned at the first sign of resistance.

"It's not what I planned," Rebecca admitted, running her fingers along the spines of books on her shelf. "But there's something powerful about navigating this unexpected turn without losing myself."

Four months into Megan's return, Rebecca had discovered something surprising. The very challenges that threatened to erase her progress had instead cemented it. Maintaining her writing practice through this disruption—even in modified form—had proven to her what intellectual understanding alone never could: that her architect identity wasn't a luxury for perfect conditions but a core aspect of who she had become.

"Before we did all this permission work," Rebecca reflected, "Megan's return would have completely derailed me. I would have packed away my writing and desk and told myself I could return to it someday, when circumstances were perfect again. But that someday might never come."

Instead, she had applied the adaptation framework, identified her non-negotiable writing hours and modified other aspects of her schedule. She created an Adult Household Agreement with Megan that respected their needs. Most importantly, she had maintained her entitled identity through the challenge.

The most powerful evidence of your transformation isn't stability during ideal circumstances but resilience during unexpected changes. Maintaining your transition architect identity when facing challenges demonstrates that your permission framework has become a fundamental part of who you are, not a temporary luxury for perfect conditions. This adaptive capability transforms you from a parent reluctantly responding to life's changes into an architect confidently designing through them.

As we conclude our journey together, the final chapter will explore how your identity transformation extends beyond your personal experience to create a lasting impact on those around you. The skills you've developed as a transition architect have prepared you to become not just the author of your next chapter, but an inspiration for others navigating their life transitions.

Conclusion: From Supporting Character to Author

Rachel stood at the bedroom doorway, her hand lingering on the light switch.

This had been Melissa's room for twenty years—walls once covered with boy-band posters, homework spread across the desk, the perpetual hint of strawberry shampoo in the air. Now it stood bare except for the guest bed and a single framed photo of Melissa's graduation. Rachel's fingers trembled slightly, not from the weight of turning off a light, but from the weight of turning toward her future.

Eight weeks ago, when we first met Rachel, she couldn't have imagined this moment of quiet power. That first night after dropping Melissa at university, Rachel had sat in her car for nearly an hour before driving home, terrified of what awaited her—not just an empty house, but an empty identity.

"Who am I if not Melissa's mother?" she had whispered into the darkness.

Today, Rachel switched off the light not with grief but with purpose. She walked down the hallway to her study—not a makeshift space crammed between laundry piles and school projects, but a room she had claimed and designed during Week Three of her permission journey. On her desk sat her Declaration of Entitlement, framed in simple wood:

I, Rachel Winters, architect of transitions, claim my rightful place as the author of my next chapter.

The Journey from Permission Deficit to Entitlement
Over these eight weeks, your path has followed a carefully designed progression, building your permission muscle through increasingly meaningful exercises. You began by acknowledging how decades of putting others first created a deep resistance to self-prioritisation—"permission deficit paralysis."

In Week One, you established your permission foundation by creating your Permission Inventory, validating your parenting accomplishments and your right to move forward. You named the guilt that surfaced whenever you considered prioritising yourself, recognising this as a normal response after years of child-focused decision-making.

During Week Two, you reclaimed small daily permissions—those 15-minute activities requiring minimal permission. Perhaps, like Rachel, you struggled with reading uninterrupted or enjoying a cup of tea without multitasking. You practised using specific permission language: "I give myself permission to walk for 15 minutes without feeling guilty."

By Week Three, you amplified your permission to more substantial domains —making space for identity exploration, creating boundary statements for key relationships, and designing your half-day permission retreat. The initial physical discomfort when prioritising yourself began to fade as your permission muscle strengthened.

In Week Four, you normalised permission through daily rituals and environmental triggers, transforming conscious effort into automatic habits. Those Post-it notes on your mirror weren't just reminders but permission anchors, retraining your brain to recognise self-prioritisation as acceptable and necessary.

Finally, you transcended permission entirely in Weeks Five through Eight, moving into genuine entitlement. You crafted your Declaration of Entitlement, developed visualisation practices, and maintained your entitled stance even when facing resistance from others or your ingrained patterns.

This journey wasn't merely about finding activities to fill time. It represented a fundamental shift in how you view yourself, from supporting character to author of your story.

Your Future as an Architect of Transitions

The architect identity you've reclaimed extends far beyond the empty nest. Michael, whom we met in Chapter 10, discovered this when facing an unexpected health diagnosis six months after his sons left for university.

"My first instinct was to hide it from the boys," he shared. "But then I caught myself slipping back into permission deficit thinking—as if my health wasn't entitled to attention and support."

Michael applied his permission framework to this new transition, moving methodically from grounding himself in what remained constant about his identity to transcending into entitled health prioritisation. The skills he developed during his empty nest transition became transferable tools for navigating this unexpected challenge.

Your future holds countless transitions:

1. Career evolution or retirement
2. Relationship changes
3. Health transitions
4. Caregiving for ageing parents
5. Geographic relocations
6. Financial shifts
7. Loss and grief
8. **New family roles, such as in-laws or grandparents**

Each transition invites you to apply your architect identity, approaching change not as a victim of circumstance but as a deliberate designer of meaningful experiences. Your permission framework provides a repeatable process for moving through uncertainty with confidence:

G - Ground yourself in what remains constant while acknowledging what's changing. R - Reclaim small daily permissions in the new context. A - Amplify permission to more significant domains affected by the transition. N - Normalise permission to enter automatic habits suitable for your new reality. T - Transcend to entitled self-direction in this new life chapter

Your Evolution from Supporting Character to Author

For decades, your days structured themselves around school schedules, sports practices, homework help, emotional support, and the thousand invisible tasks of active parenting. You measured your success primarily by how well you supported others in achieving their goals.

You've reclaimed your right to centre stage in your life story. Your permission journey has transformed you from:

- Waiting for external validation → Self-authorisation
- Permission-seeking → Entitled self-direction

- Guilt when prioritising yourself → Confidence in your right to self-care
- Defining worth through service → Valuing your inherent worth
- Reacting to others' needs → Proactively designing your life
- Supporting character → Author

This evolution hasn't diminished your relationships with your adult children. Jennifer, whom we met in Chapter 12, discovered that her daughter responded with unexpected admiration to her mother's transformation:

"Mom, seeing you build this new life makes me less afraid of growing up," her daughter told her. "I used to worry that adulthood was all about loss, but watching you learn painting shows me that we keep growing our whole lives."

You haven't abandoned your parenting legacy by reclaiming your right to author your next chapter—you've extended it. You've shown your children that healthy adulthood includes continuous growth and self-renewal.

Your Continued Growth and Expansion

The permission journey doesn't end here. Your permission muscle requires ongoing development through:

1. **Regular review of your Declaration of Entitlement.** Post it where you'll see it daily, revising it as your confidence grows.
2. **Quarterly permission assessments.** Schedule time every three months to evaluate how consistently you maintain your entitlement mindset and identify areas needing attention.
3. **Active application to new transitions.** Practice your architect skills on minor life changes before major transitions arise.
4. **Permission accountability partnerships**: Connect with others working to overcome the permission deficit, sharing practices and challenges.
5. **Ongoing documentation:** Continue your permission journal, recording evidence of your growing entitlement capabilities.
6. **Permission extension to others**: Help others recognise and overcome their permission deficit.
7. **Expanded architect toolkit:** Seek additional resources on navigating transitions with intention.

Remember that transformation isn't a destination but an ongoing journey. You'll still experience moments of permission deficit, particularly during stress or new transitions. Return to the GRANT framework when this happens, starting with whatever step feels most accessible.

Ten months after her daughter left for university, Rachel faced an unexpected opportunity—a writing retreat in Tuscany. Her first thought was, "I couldn't possibly..." But then she caught herself, laughed, and reached for her journal.

"I've been building this permission muscle for nearly a year," she wrote. "Time to see what it can lift."

She booked the retreat that afternoon.

She sat in her sunlit study four days later, writing her first chapter. It is not the first chapter of a novel, though it will come later. She was writing the first chapter of her subsequent life phase—a chapter where she moved beyond permission entirely, into the entitled authority of an author who knows her story matters.

Your identity was never just "parent" but always the architect of meaningful transitions. The empty nest that once felt like an ending has become your beginning—the first chapter in your entitled self-direction story.

The page has turned. The pen is in your hand. Begin.

Appendices: Your Permission-Based Transformation Toolkit

Sarah stared at the blank permission statement on her desk, pen hovering uncertainly above the paper.

After twenty-three years of putting her children first, writing "I give myself permission to..." felt like trying to speak a foreign language. Her hand trembled slightly—the physical manifestation of her permission deficit. Then she flipped to Appendix A of this book, found the template that resonated with her situation, and began writing with newfound clarity. Two months later, she would describe this moment as the true beginning of her entitled self-direction. Like Sarah, these appendices aren't mere supplements but essential companions on your permission journey—practical tools that transform abstract concepts into daily practices.

Appendix A: Permission Statement Templates

Despite her husband's enthusiastic support, Elena couldn't understand why she felt guilty about taking an art class.

The intellectual understanding was there—of course, she deserved to explore her creativity now that the kids were gone—but the emotional authorisation was missing. When she discovered the permission statement templates, she found language for what had previously been an unnamed barrier. "I fully authorise myself to invest time and money in my artistic development without requiring external validation," she wrote, following the Amplification Permission template. By speaking these words aloud each morning before her class, she gradually silenced the guilt voice that had kept her creatively paralysed for decades.

These templates form the verbal foundation of your permission practice, organised into five progressive categories matching the GRANT framework:

1. **Foundational Permission Statements** help beginners take initial steps with minimal resistance
2. **Recovery Permission Statements** support reclaiming small moments throughout your day
3. **Amplification Permission Statements** expand permission into meaningful identity areas
4. **Normalisation Permission Statements** transform conscious effort into automatic habits
5. **Transcendence Declarations** establish entitled self-direction as your new normal

Each template includes customisation points for your specific situation and guidance on delivery—whether spoken aloud, written, or both. Begin with foundational statements that trigger minimal guilt and gradually progress toward transcendence declarations. The incremental approach builds your permission muscle without overwhelming your emotional system.

Keep these templates accessible during challenging moments when the right words make the difference between action and paralysis.

Appendix B: Weekly Schedule Design Tools

Michael found himself wandering his empty house at 10 AM on a Tuesday, coffee cup in hand, with no idea how to fill the next eight hours.

After decades of his schedule being dictated by his children's needs, the freedom felt more like floating in space than liberation. The weekly schedule templates provided the gravitational pull he needed—not restrictive timetables but flexible architectures that gave just enough structure to prevent anxiety while honouring his newfound freedom. "I'm not just filling hours," he told friends, "I'm building a life with intention."

These tools address the Time Wealth Paradox by transforming time anxiety into purposeful design across four essential quadrants:

1. **Purpose: Activities** for meaningful work, learning, and creative expression

2. **Relationship Investments** balanced across adult children, partner, friends, and community
3. **Contribution Opportunities** for wisdom-sharing and value-aligned service
4. **Self-Care Foundations** that protect time for physical, emotional, and spiritual renewal

You'll find weekly frameworks, daily ritual planners, flexibility matrices for handling unexpected events, energy mapping tools to align activities with your natural rhythms, and permission integration checkpoints that remind you to practice self-authorisation throughout your day.

Multiple template versions accommodate different lifestyles, whether you're working full-time, part-time, or focusing entirely on your next chapter design. Begin with the structure that most closely matches your current situation, then adapt it as your comfort with time architecture grows.

Appendix C: The Complete GRANT System Quick Reference

Jennifer kept the GRANT Quick Reference guide on her nightstand, consulting it during moments of uncertainty.

Six weeks into her permission journey, she hit an emotional wall—her daughter announced a surprise visit home from college, triggering old caregiving patterns that threatened to derail her progress. Rather than abandoning her permission practice, Jennifer consulted the troubleshooting section, which offered specific strategies for maintaining boundaries during family visits. The visit became an opportunity to practice her evolving identity rather than a regression to old patterns.

This condensed road map keeps you oriented during emotional fluctuations with:

1. **Week-by-Week Action Steps** that clarify exactly what to do each week
2. **Daily Practice Guides** that build consistent permission habits
3. **Progression Benchmarks** to assess your permission development
4. **Troubleshooting Solutions** for Common Challenges
5. **Emotional Response Tracking** tools to document and analyse your reactions

6. **Integration Checkpoints** to ensure each step builds on previous progress
7. **Permission Scope Expansion** guidelines for gradually increasing domains

Each page follows a consistent format, featuring clear headings, actionable steps, and progress tracking tools. Colour coding helps you quickly identify which stage of the GRANT framework you're working in. Keep this reference accessible as a constant reminder of your progress and next steps.

Appendix D: Recommended Resources for Identity Exploration

After three decades of identifying primarily as "Mark and Kyle's mom," Diane struggled to answer when asked about her interests.

Her permission journal revealed progress in self-authorisation but little clarity about what she wanted to authorise herself to do—the identity exploration resources provided structured pathways for discovering her post-parenting self. A values assessment revealed her core priorities had shifted since her twenties. At the same time, a creative exploratory workshop helped her rediscover a passion for environmental advocacy that had been dormant since before her children were born.

This curated resource library includes:

1. **Books and Readings** addressing empty nest psychology and identity transformation
2. **Online Communities** where empty nesters share experiences and strategies
3. **Assessment Tools** for clarifying values, interests, and purpose possibilities
4. **Professional Services** guidelines for selecting appropriate support
5. **Creative Exploration Resources** offering arts-based approaches to identity discovery
6. **Digital Applications** supporting permission practices and time architecture
7. **Relationship Evolution Resources** for transforming family and social connections

Each recommendation includes a brief description, appropriate timing within your 8-week journey, and guidance for extracting maximum value.

Resources are rated on their alignment with the GRANT framework and their effectiveness for different stages of permission development.

While the GRANT system provides everything needed for success, these additional resources connect you with others on similar journeys, filling the gap left by limited cultural frameworks for the empty nest transition.

Appendix E: Glossary of Permission Framework Terms

During her first meeting of the empty nest support group, Rachel struggled to articulate her experience.

"I should enjoy this freedom, but I need... permission? That sounds ridiculous," she said hesitantly. Another member nodded and replied, "That's called a permission deficit—it's when you intellectually know you deserve to prioritise yourself, but emotionally, you can't do it without authorisation." The relief of having precise language to describe her experience was visible on Rachel's face. "Yes! That's exactly it!" she exclaimed, suddenly feeling less alone.

This comprehensive glossary provides clear definitions of all specialised terminology used throughout the book, including:

1. **Permission Deficit**: The psychological state of requiring external authorisation despite intellectual understanding
2. **Transition Architect**: Your fundamental identity as someone who designs meaningful life transitions
3. **Time Wealth Paradox**: How abundance of unstructured time creates more anxiety than scarcity
4. **Permission Muscle**: The psychological capability that strengthens through progressive exercises
5. **Entitled Self-Direction**: The evolved state beyond permission-seeking to automatic self-prioritisation
6. **Identity Archaeology**: The process of excavating pre-parenting passions and interests
7. **Permission Inventory**: Documentation of current self-authorisation patterns
8. **Environmental Permission Triggers**: Physical reminders prompting permission practices

Each definition includes the term, meaning within the GRANT framework, practical examples, and cross-references to related concepts. Studies show that precise language to describe psychological experiences significantly increases our ability to transform them. This glossary provides you with the necessary linguistic precision.

As you begin your permission-based transformation, these appendices provide the practical tools to move from concept to daily practice. When Marcus found himself hesitating to join a hiking club six weeks after his daughter left for college, he didn't just remember the concept of permission deficit—he pulled out his personalised statement template, consulted his weekly schedule design, and checked the GRANT quick reference for guidance. The tools made his permission journey concrete and actionable. Your journey to becoming the architect of your next chapter becomes both intellectually understood and practically implemented through these resources, which bridge the gap between concept and living practice.

Reader Reviews for "Empty Nest Transformation"

Share Your Transformation Journey!

THANK you for completing "Empty Nest Transformation: The 8-Week System to Rebuild Identity, Create Daily Purpose, and Design Your Next Chapter Without Paralysing Guilt." We hope this book has helped you navigate this significant life transition with greater confidence and purpose.

We'd love to hear about your experience! Your feedback helps other empty nesters find this resource and creates a supportive community of fellow architects of meaningful transitions.

Share Your Story

- What was your biggest takeaway from the GRANT Permission Escalation System?
- Which chapter or exercise created the most significant shift in your thinking?
- How has your relationship with yourself changed since implementing these practices?
- What advice would you give to someone just starting their empty nest journey?

What Readers Are Saying

★★★★★ "Permission to Thrive" - *Margaret T., 54*
"After 22 years of putting my three children first, I couldn't even sit down to read a book without feeling guilty. The Permission Inventory exercise was a revelation—I realised I'd been waiting for someone to permit me to exist beyond motherhood. Now I'm not only permitting myself, I'm claiming it as my right. My adult children respect me more for it!"

★★★★★ "From Co-Parents to Partners Again" - *David & Janet K., 56 & 55*
"Our marriage had become a logistical operation revolving around our kids. The Marriage Renaissance chapter gave us practical tools to rediscover each other. The couple of ritual suggestions led to our 'Thursday Explorations'—we take turns planning an evening doing something new each week. We're connecting in ways we haven't in decades."

★★★★★ "The Architect of My Second Act" - *Susan M., 49*
"The 'transition architect' concept completely reframed how I saw myself. I wasn't just losing my identity as a mom—I was gaining the opportunity to apply those same skills to designing my next chapter. I've started a community arts program using the exact organisational talents I developed coordinating my kids' activities. The Declaration of Entitlement hangs framed in my office as a daily reminder."

★★★★ "Time Structure That Feels Like Freedom" - *Robert L., 58*
"The time architecture templates transformed my relationship with unstructured time. After decades of cramming personal interests into scattered moments between my children's needs, the abundance of time triggered anxiety. Creating intentional structure using the purpose portfolio approach has given me both direction and flexibility. Four stars only because I would have appreciated more examples for those of us who still work full-time."

★★★★★ "The Permission Deficit Was My Invisible Barrier" - *Elena R., 51*
"I've read three empty nest books that told me to 'find a hobby' or 'rediscover myself'—but none addressed why I physically couldn't follow through. This

book nailed it: the concept of permission deficit paralysis. The progressive permission exercises were effective when nothing else was, because they addressed the actual psychological barrier. I started with five minutes of uninterrupted reading and built to launching my consulting business. Life-changing doesn't begin to cover it."

Submit Your Review
We welcome your honest feedback! Please consider leaving a review on:

- Amazon
- Goodreads
- Barnes & Noble
- Your social media

"Your identity was never just a parent but always the architect of meaningful transitions."

Lily Wright

Printed in Dunstable, United Kingdom